The Death of Sex and the Demise of Monogamy

By: Sam Vaknin

I. The New Normal

Whatever Happened to Marriage?

The ancient institution of monogamous marriage is ill-suited to the exigencies of modern Western civilization. People of both genders live and work longer (which renders monogamy impracticable); travel far and away frequently; and are exposed to tempting romantic alternatives via social networking and in various workplace and social settings.

Thus, even as social monogamy and pair commitment and bonding are still largely intact and more condoned than ever and eve as infidelity is fervently condemned, sexual exclusivity (mislabelled "sexual monogamy") is declining, especially among the young and the old. Monogamy is becoming one alternative of many lifestyles and marriage only one relationship among a few (sometimes, not even a privileged or unique relationship, as it competes for time and resources with work, same-sex friends, friends with benefits, and opposite-sex friends.)

The contractual aspects of marriage are more pronounced than ever with everything on the table: from extramarital sex (allowed or not) to pre-nuptial agreements. The commodification and preponderance of sex – premarital and extramarital - robbed it of its function as a conduit of specialness and intimacy and since childrearing is largely avoided (natality rates are precipitously plummeting everywhere) or outsourced, the family has lost both its raison d'etre and its nature as the venue for exclusive sexual and emotional interactions between adults.

Professed values and prevailing social mores and institutions have yet to catch up to this emerging multifarious reality. The consequences of these discrepancies are disastrous: about 40-50% of all first-time marriages end in divorce and the percentage is much higher for second and third attempts at connubial bliss. Open communication about one's sexual needs is tantamount to self-ruination as one's partner is likely to reflexively initiate a divorce. Dishonesty and cheating are definitely the rational choices in such an unforgiving and punitive environment.

Indeed, most surviving marriages have to do with perpetuating the partners' convenience, their access to commonly-owned assets and future streams of income, and the welfare of third parties, most notably their kids. Erstwhile sexual exclusivity often degenerates into celibacy or abstinence on the one hand – or parallel lives with multiple sexual and emotional partners on the other hand.

One night stands for both genders are usually opportunistic. Extra-pair affairs are self-limiting, as emotional involvement and sexual attraction wane over time. Infidelity is, therefore, much less of a threat to the longevity of a dedicated couple than it is made out to be. Most of the damage is caused by culturally-conditioned, albeit deeply and traumatically felt, reactions to conduct that is almost universally decried as deceitful, dishonest, and in breach of vows and promises.

But the roots of the crumbling alliance between men and women go deeper and further in time. Long before divorce became a social norm, men and women grew into two disparate, incompatible, and warring subspecies. Traditionalist, conservative, and religious societies put in place behavioural safeguards against the inevitable wrenching torsion that monogamy entailed: no premarital sex (virginity); no multiple intimate partners; no cohabitation prior to tying the knot; no mobility, or equal rights for women; no mixing of the genders. We now know that each of these habits does, indeed, increase the chances for an ultimate divorce. As Jonathan Franzen elucidates in his literary masterpieces, it boils down to a choice between personal freedoms and the stability of the family: the former decisively preclude the latter.

During the 17th, 18th, and 19th centuries, discreet affairs were an institution of marriage: sexual gratification and emotional intimacy were outsourced while all other domestic functions were shared in partnership. The Industrial Revolution, the Victorian Age, the backlash of the sexual revolution, belligerent feminism, and the advent of socially-atomizing and gender-equalizing transportation, information processing, and telecommunication technologies led inexorably to the hollowing out of family and hearth.

In a civilization centred on brainpower, Men have lost the relative edge that brawn used to provide. Monogamy is increasingly considered as past its expiry date: a historical aberration that reflects the economic and political realities of bygone eras. Moreover: the incidence of lifelong singlehood has skyrocketed as people hope for their potential or actual relationship-partners to provide for all their sexual, emotional, social, and economic needs – and then get sorely disappointed when they fail to meet these highly unrealistic expectations.

In an age of economic self-sufficiency, electronic entertainment, and self-gratification, the art of compromise in relationships is gone. Single motherhood (sometimes via IVF, with no identifiable partner involved) has become the norm in many countries. Even within marriages or committed relationships, solitary pursuits, such as separate vacations, or "girls'/boy' nights out" have become the norm.

The 20th century was a monument to male fatuity: wars and ideologies almost decimated the species. Forced to acquire masculine skills and fill men's shoes in factories and fields, women discovered militant self-autonomy, the superfluousness of men, and the untenability of the male claims to superiority over them.

In an age of malignant individualism, bordering on narcissism, men and women alike put themselves, their fantasies, and their needs first, all else – family included – be damned. And with 5 decades of uninterrupted prosperity, birth control, and feminism/ women's lib most of the female denizens of the West have acquired the financial wherewithal to realize their dreams at the expense and to the detriment of collectives they ostensibly belong to (such as the nuclear family.) Feminism is a movement focused on negatives (obliterating women's age-old bondage) but it offers few constructive ideas regarding women's new roles. By casting men as the enemy, it also failed to educate them and convert them into useful allies.

Owing to the dramatic doubling of life expectancy, modern marriages seem to go through three phases: infatuation (honeymoon); procreation-accumulation (of assets, children, and shared experiences); and exhaustion-outsourcing (bonding with new emotional and sexual partners for rejuvenation or the fulfilment of long-repressed fantasies, needs, and wishes.) Divorces and breakups occur mostly at the seams, the periods of transition between these phases and especially between the stages of accumulation-procreation and exhaustion-outsourcing. This is where family units break down.

With marriage on the decline and infidelity on the rise, the reasonable solution would be swinging (swapping sexual partners) or polyamory (households with multiple partners of both genders all of whom are committed to one another for the long haul, romantically-involved, sexually-shared, and economically united.) Alas, while a perfectly rational development of the traditional marriage and one that is best-suited to modernity, it is an emotionally unstable arrangement, what with romantic jealousy ineluctably rearing its ugly head. Very few people are emotionally capable of sharing their life-partner with others.

Human psychology dictates that in any modern, adaptable variant of marriage monogamy must be preserved while allowing for emotional, sexual, and romantic diversity. How to square the circle? What virtual chastity belt can we conjure up to replace the spiked medieval original?

Enter "time-limited marriages" (TLM). These are marriage contracts with expiration dates: one to three years for childless couples and a minimum of seven years for those blessed with children (to allow the parents to provide a stable environment during the child's formative years.) These contracts can be allowed to expire and then the parties are free to look elsewhere for the fulfilment of their sexual and romantic dreams and wishes; or they can be renewed and renegotiated.

The question is not why there are so many divorces, but why so few. Surely, serial monogamy (in effect, a tawdry variant of TLM) is far better, fairer, and more humane than adultery? Couples stay together and tolerate straying owing to inertia; financial or emotional dependence; insecurity (lack of self-confidence or low self-esteem); fear of the unknown and the tedium of dating. Some couples persevere owing to religious conviction of for the sake of appearances. Yet others make a smooth transition to an alternative lifestyle (polyamory, swinging, or consensual adultery).

Indeed, what has changed is not the incidence of adultery, even among women. There are good grounds to assume that it has remained the same throughout human history. The phenomenon - quantitatively and qualitatively - has always been the same, merely underreported. What have changed are the social acceptability of extramarital sex both before and during marriage and the ease of obtaining divorce. People discuss adultery openly where before it was a taboo topic.

Another new development may be the rise of "selfish affairs" among women younger than 35 who are used to multiple sexual partners. "Selfish affairs" are acts of recreational adultery whose sole purpose is to satisfy sexual curiosity and the need for romantic diversity. The emotional component in these usually short-term affairs (one-night stands and the like) is muted. Among women older than 60, adultery has become the accepted way of seeking emotional connection and intimacy outside the marital bond. These are "outsourcing affairs."

Within the TLM, partners would have little incentive to cheat: they could simply wait for the contract to lapse. The looming expiry would also keep the intimate partners on their toes and on their best behavior by generating a sempiternal environment of courtship and positive sexual tension. The periodically renegotiated marriage contracts would reflect changing economic realities, shifts in romantic sentiment, and other pertinent new data. Of course, TLM would eliminate the need for divorces (except in extreme, emergency cases.)

Until recently, couples formed around promises of emotional exclusivity and sexual fidelity, uniqueness in each other's mind and life, and (more common until the 1940s) virginity. Marriage was also a partnership: economic, or related to childrearing, or companionship. It was based on the partners' past and background and geared towards a shared future.

Nowadays, couples coalesce around the twin undertakings of continuity ("I will ALWAYS be there for you") and availability ("I will always BE there for you.") Issues of exclusivity, uniqueness, and virginity have been relegated to the back-burner. It is no longer practical to demand of one's spouse to have nothing to do with the opposite sex, not to spend the bulk of his or her time outside the marriage, not to take separate vacations, and, more generally, to be joined at the hip. Affairs, for instance – both emotional and sexual – are sad certainties in the life of every couple.

Members of the couple are supposed to make themselves continuously available to each other and to provide emotional sustenance and support in an atmosphere of sharing, companionship, and friendship. All the traditional functions of the family can now be – and often are – outsourced, including even sex and emotional intimacy. But, contrary to marriage, outsourcing is frequently haphazard and unpredictable, dependent as it is on outsiders who are committed elsewhere as well. Hence the relative durability of marriage, in its conservative and less-conventional forms alike: it is a convenient and highly practicable arrangement.

Divorce or other forms of marital breakup are not new phenomena. But their precipitants have undergone a revolutionary shift. In the past, families fell apart owing to a breach of exclusivity, mainly in the forms of emotional or sexual infidelity; a deficiency of uniqueness and primacy: divorced women, for instance, were considered "damaged goods" because they used to "belong" to another man and, therefore, could offer neither primacy nor uniqueness; or an egregious violation of the terms of partnership (for example: sloth, dysfunctional childrearing, infertility).

Nowadays, intimate partners bail out when the continuous availability of their significant others is disrupted: sexually, emotionally, or as friends and companions. Marriages are about the present and are being put to the test on a daily basis. Partners who are dissatisfied opt out and team up with other, more promising providers. Children are serially reared by multiple parents and in multiple households.

Still, despite all the fashionable theories of marriage, the narratives and the feminists, the reasons to get married largely remain the same. True, there have been role reversals and new stereotypes have cropped up. But biological, physiological and biochemical facts are less amenable to modern criticisms of culture. Men are still men and women are still women.

Men and women marry to form:

The Sexual Dyad – Intended to gratify the partners' sexual attraction and secure a stable, consistent and available source of sexual gratification.

The Economic Dyad – The couple is a functioning economic unit within which the economic activities of the members of the dyad and of additional entrants are carried out. The economic unit generates more wealth than it consumes and the synergy between its members is likely to lead to gains in production and in productivity relative to individual efforts and investments.

The Social Dyad – The members of the couple bond as a result of implicit or explicit, direct, or indirect social pressures. Such pressure can manifest itself in numerous forms. In Judaism, a person cannot hold some religious posts unless he is married. This is a form of economic pressure.

In most human societies, avowed bachelors are considered to be socially deviant and abnormal. They are condemned by society, ridiculed, shunned and isolated, effectively ex-communicated. Partly to avoid these sanctions and partly to enjoy the emotional glow that comes with conformity and acceptance, couples get married.

Today, myriad lifestyles are on offer. The old fashioned, nuclear family is one of many variants. Children are reared by single parents. Homosexual couples bind and abound. But a pattern is discernible all the same: almost 95% of the adult population get married ultimately. They settle into a two-member arrangement, whether formalized and sanctioned religiously or legally – or not.

The Companionship Dyad – Formed by adults in search of sources of long-term and stable support, emotional warmth, empathy, care, good advice and intimacy. The members of these couples tend to define themselves as each other's best friends.

Folk wisdom tells us that the first three dyads are unstable.

Sexual attraction wanes and is replaced by sexual attrition in most cases. This could lead to the adoption of non-conventional sexual behavior patterns (sexual abstinence, group sex, couple swapping, etc.) – or to recurrent marital infidelity.

Pecuniary concerns are insufficient grounds for a lasting relationship, either. In today's world, both partners are potentially financially independent. This new found autonomy gnaws at the roots of traditional patriarchal-domineering-disciplinarian relationships. Marriage is becoming a more balanced, business like, arrangement with children and the couple's welfare and life standard as its products.

Thus, marriages motivated solely by economic considerations are as likely to unravel as any other joint venture. Admittedly, social pressures help maintain family cohesiveness and stability. But – being thus enforced from the outside – such marriages resemble detention rather than a voluntary, joyful collaboration.

Moreover, social norms, peer pressure, and social conformity cannot be relied upon to fulfil the roles of stabilizer and shock absorber indefinitely. Norms change and peer pressure can backfire ("If all my friends are divorced and apparently content, why shouldn't I try it, too ?").

Only the companionship dyad seems to be durable. Friendships deepen with time. While sex loses its initial, biochemically-induced, lustre, economic motives are reversed or voided, and social norms are fickle – companionship, like wine, improves with time.

Even when planted on the most desolate land, under the most difficult and insidious circumstances, the obdurate seed of companionship sprouts and blossoms.

"Matchmaking is made in heaven" goes the old Jewish adage but Jewish matchmakers in centuries past were not averse to lending the divine a hand. After closely scrutinizing the background of both candidates – male and female – a marriage was pronounced. In other cultures, marriages are still being arranged by prospective or actual fathers without asking for the embryos or the toddlers' consent.

The surprising fact is that arranged marriages last much longer than those which are the happy outcomes of romantic love. Moreover: the longer a couple cohabitates prior to their marriage, the higher the likelihood of divorce. Counterintuitively, romantic love and cohabitation ("getting to know each other better") are negative precursors and predictors of marital longevity.

Companionship grows out of friction and interaction within an irreversible formal arrangement (no "escape clauses"). In many marriages where divorce is not an option (legally, or due to prohibitive economic or social costs), companionship grudgingly develops and with it contentment, if not happiness.

Companionship is the offspring of pity and empathy. It is based on and shared events and fears and common suffering. It reflects the wish to protect and to shield each other from the hardships of life. It is habit forming. If lustful sex is fire – companionship is old slippers: comfortable, static, useful, warm, and secure.

Experiments and experience show that people in constant touch get attached to one another very quickly and very thoroughly. This is a reflex that has to do with survival. As infants, we get attached to other mothers and our mothers get attached to us. In the absence of social interactions, we die younger. We need to bond and to make others depend on us in order to survive.

The mating (and, later, marital) cycle is full of euphorias and dysphorias. These "mood swings" generate the dynamics of seeking mates, copulating, coupling (marrying) and reproducing.

The source of these changing dispositions can be found in the meaning that we attach to marriage which is perceived as the real, irrevocable, irreversible and serious entry into adult society. Previous rites of passage (like the Jewish Bar Mitzvah, the Christian Communion and more exotic rites elsewhere) prepare us only partially to the shocking realization that we are about to emulate our parents.

During the first years of our lives, we tend to view our parents as omnipotent, omniscient, and omnipresent demigods. Our perception of them, of ourselves and of the world is magical. All entities - we and our caregivers included - are entangled, constantly interacting, and identity interchanging ("shape shifting").

At first, therefore, our parents are idealized. Then, as we get disillusioned, they are internalized to become the first and most important among the inner voices that guide our lives. As we grow up (adolescence) we rebel against our parents (in the final phases of identity formation) and then learn to accept them and to resort to them in times of need.

But the primordial gods of our infancy never die, nor do they lie dormant. They lurk in our superego, engaged in incessant dialogue with the other structures of our personality. They constantly criticize and analyze, make suggestions and reproach. The hiss of these voices is the background radiation of our personal big bang.

Thus, to decide to get married (to imitate our parents), is to challenge and tempt the gods, to commit sacrilege, to negate the very existence of our progenitors, to defile the inner sanctum of our formative years. This is a rebellion so momentous, so all encompassing, that it touches upon the very foundation of our personality.

Inevitably, we (unconsciously) shudder in anticipation of the imminent and, no doubt, horrible punishment that awaits us for this iconoclastic presumptuousness. This is the first dysphoria, which accompanies our mental preparations prior to getting wed. Getting ready to get hitched carries a price tag: the activation of a host of primitive and hitherto dormant defence mechanisms - denial, regression, repression, projection.

This self-induced panic is the result of an inner conflict. On the one hand, we know that it is unhealthy to live as recluses (both biologically and psychologically). With the passage of time, we are urgently propelled to find a mate. On the other hand, there is the above-described feeling of impending doom.

Having overcome the initial anxiety, having triumphed over our inner tyrants (or guides, depending on the character of the primary objects, their parents), we go through a short euphoric phase, celebrating their rediscovered individuation and separation. Reinvigorated, we feel ready to court and woo prospective mates.

But our conflicts are never really put to rest. They merely lie dormant.

Married life is a terrifying rite of passage. Many react to it by limiting themselves to familiar, knee-jerk behavior patterns and reactions and by ignoring or dimming their true emotions. Gradually, these marriages are hollowed out and wither.

Some seek solace in resorting to other frames of reference - the terra cognita of one's neighbourhood, country, language, race, culture, language, background, profession, social stratum, or education. Belonging to these groups imbues them with feelings of security and firmness.

Many combine both solutions. More than 80% of marriages take place among members of the same social class, profession, race, creed and breed. This is not a chance statistic. It reflects choices, conscious and (more often) unconscious.

The next anti-climatic dysphoric phase transpires when our attempts to secure (the consent of) a mate are met with success. Daydreaming is easier and more gratifying than the dreariness of realized goals. Mundane routine is the enemy of love and of optimism. Where dreams end, harsh reality intrudes with its uncompromising demands.

Securing the consent of one's future spouse forces one to tread an irreversible and increasingly challenging path. One's imminent marriage requires not only emotional investment - but also economic and social ones. Many people fear commitment and feel trapped, shackled, or even threatened. Marriage suddenly seems like a dead end. Even those eager to get married entertain occasional and nagging doubts.

The strength of these negative emotions depends, to a very large extent, on the parental role models and on the kind of family life experienced. The more dysfunctional the family of origin - the earlier (and usually only) available example – the more overpowering the sense of entrapment and the resulting paranoia and backlash.

But most people overcome this stage fright and proceed to formalize their relationship by getting married. This decision, this leap of faith is the corridor which leads to the palatial hall of post-nuptial euphoria.

This time the euphoria is mostly a social reaction. The newly conferred status (of "just married") bears a cornucopia of social rewards and incentives, some of them enshrined in legislation. Economic benefits, social approval, familial support, the envious reactions of others, the expectations and joys of marriage (freely available sex, having children, lack of parental or societal control, and newly experienced freedoms) foster another magical bout of feeling omnipotent.

It feels good and empowering to control one's newfound "lebensraum", one's spouse, and one's life. It fosters self-confidence, self esteem and helps regulate one's sense of self-worth. It is a manic phase. Everything seems possible, now that one is left to one's own devices and is supported by one's mate.

With luck and the right partner, this frame of mind can be prolonged. However, as life's disappointments accumulate, obstacles mount, the possible sorted out from the improbable and time passes inexorably, this euphoria abates. The reserves of energy and determination dwindle. Gradually, one slides into an all-pervasive dysphoric (even anhedonic or depressed) mood.

The routines of life, its mundane attributes, the contrast between fantasy and reality, erode the first burst of exuberance. Life looks more like a life sentence. This anxiety sours the relationship. One tends to blame one's spouse for one's atrophy. People with alloplastic defences (external locus of control) blame others for their defeats and failures.

Thoughts of breaking free, of going back to the parental nest, of revoking the marriage become more frequent. It is, at the same time, a frightening and exhilarating prospect. Again, panic sets it. Conflict rears its ugly head. Cognitive dissonance abounds. Inner turmoil leads to irresponsible, self-defeating and self-destructive behaviours. A lot of marriages end here in what is known as the "seven year itch".

Next awaits parenthood. Many marriages survive only because of the presence of common offspring.

One cannot become a parent unless and until one eradicates the internal traces of one's own parents. This necessary patricide and unavoidable matricide are painful and cause great trepidation. But the completion of this crucial phase is rewarding all the same and it leads to feelings of renewed vigour, new-found optimism, a sensation of omnipotence and the reawakening of other traces of magical thinking.

In the quest for an outlet, a way to relieve anxiety and boredom, both members of the couple (providing they still possess the wish to "save" the marriage) hit upon the same idea but from different directions.

The woman (partly because of social and cultural conditioning during the socialization process) finds bringing children to the world an attractive and efficient way of securing the bond, cementing the relationship and transforming it into a long-term commitment. Pregnancy, childbirth, and motherhood are perceived as the ultimate manifestations of her femininity.

The male reaction to childrearing is more compounded. At first, he perceives the child (at least unconsciously) as another restraint, likely to only "drag him deeper" into the quagmire. His dysphoria deepens and matures into full-fledged panic. It then subsides and gives way to a sense of awe and wonder. A psychedelic feeling of being part parent (to the child) and part child (to his own parents) ensues. The birth of the child and his first stages of development only serve to entrench this "time warp" impression.

Raising children is a difficult task. It is time and energy consuming. It is emotionally taxing. It denies the parent his or her privacy, intimacy, and needs. The newborn represents a full-blown traumatic crisis with potentially devastating consequences. The strain on the relationship is enormous. It either completely breaks down – or is revived by the novel challenges and hardships.

An euphoric period of collaboration and reciprocity, of mutual support and increasing love follows. Everything else pales beside the little miracle. The child becomes the centre of narcissistic projections, hopes and fears. So much is vested and invested in the infant and, initially, the child gives so much in return that it blots away the daily problems, tedious routines, failures, disappointments and aggravations of every normal relationship.

But the child's role is temporary. The more autonomous s/he becomes, the more knowledgeable, the less innocent – the less rewarding and the more frustrating s/he is. As toddlers become adolescents, many couples fall apart, their members having grown apart, developed separately and are estranged.

The stage is set for the next major dysphoria: the midlife crisis.

This, essentially, is a crisis of reckoning, of inventory taking, disillusionment, the realization of one's mortality. We look back to find how little we had accomplished, how short the time we have left, how unrealistic our expectations have been, how alienated we have become, how ill-equipped we are to cope, and how irrelevant and unhelpful our marriages are.

To the disenchanted midlifer, his life is a fake, a Potemkin village, a facade behind which rot and corruption have consumed his vitality. This seems to be the last chance to recover lost ground, to strike one more time. Invigorated by other people's youth (a young lover, one's students or colleagues, one's own children), one tries to recreate one's life in a vain attempt to make amends, and to avoid the same mistakes.

This crisis is exacerbated by the "empty nest" syndrome (as children grow up and leave the parents' home). A major topic of consensus and a catalyst of interaction thus disappear. The vacuity of the relationship engendered by the termites of a thousand marital discords is revealed.

This hollowness can be filled with empathy and mutual support. It rarely is, however. Most couples discover that they lost faith in their powers of rejuvenation and that their togetherness is buried under a mountain of grudges, regrets and sorrows.

They both want out. And out they go. The majority of those who do remain married revert to cohabitation rather than to love, to co-existence rather to experimentation, to arrangements of convenience rather to an emotional revival. It is a sad sight. As biological decay sets in, the couple heads into the ultimate dysphoria: ageing and death.

Divorce as a Re-Distributive Mechanism

"Even in modern times, in most cases husbands and wives differ in their potential for acquiring property. In separation of property, husbands and wives owning property and dealing with each other will be in the same position as unmarried adults.

There are, however, grounds for distinguishing marital property questions from ordinary property questions, because persons who cohabit on a domestic basis share a common standard of living and usually also the benefits of each other's property. A major element in many marriages is the raising of children, and the traditional female role, requiring her full-time presence in the home, places the married woman at a disadvantage so far as earning money and acquiring property are concerned. It is inconsistent of society to encourage a woman to take the domestic role of wife and mother, with its lower money and property potential, but in property matters to treat her as if she were a single person. It is also inconsistent to place upon the husband the sole responsibility for maintaining his wife and children, if his wife has regular employment outside the home. When the marriage is dissolved, if the wife has not been regularly employed and now enters the labour market on a full-time basis, she may be at a considerable disadvantage as far as salary and pension rights are concerned."

Encyclopaedia Britannica, 1997 Edition

When a man and a woman dissolve their marriage, matters of common matrimonial property are often settled by dividing between them the assets generated and accumulated by one or both of them during the marriage. How the property is divided depends on the law prevailing in their domicile and upon the existence of a prenuptial contract.

The question is legally exceedingly intricate and requires specific expertise that far exceeds anything this author has to offer. It is the economic angle that is intriguing.

Divorce in modern times constitutes one of the biggest transfers of wealth in the annals of Mankind. Amounts of cash and assets, which dwarf anything OPEC used to have in its heyday, pass between spouses yearly. Most of the beneficiaries are women. Because the earning power of men is almost double that of women (depending on the country) – most of the wealth accumulated by any couple is directly traceable to the husband's income. A divorce, therefore, constitutes a transfer of part of the husband's wealth to his wife. Because the cumulative disparities over years of income differentials are great – the wealth transferred is enormous.

Consider a husband that makes an average of US $40,000 after-tax annually throughout his working years. He is likely to save c. $1,000 annually (net savings in the USA prior to 1995 averaged 2.5% of disposable income). This is close to US $8,000 in 7 years with interest and dividends reinvested and assuming no appreciation in the prices of financial assets.

His wife stands to receive half of these savings (c. $4,000) if the marriage is dissolved after 7 years. Had she started to work at the same time as her husband and continued to do so for 7 years as well – on average, she will have earned 60% of his income.

Assuming an identical savings rate for her, she would have saved only US $5,000 and her husband would be entitled to US $2,500 of it. Thus, a net transfer of US $1,500 in cash from husband to wife is one of the the likely outcomes of the divorce of this very typical couple.

But this ignores the transfer of tangible and intangible assets from husband to wife. A seven year old couple in the West typically owns $100,000 in assets. When they divorce, by splitting the assets right down the middle, the man actually transfers to the woman about $10,000 in assets, taking their income differential into account.

An average of 45% of the couples in the Western hemisphere end up divorcing within 7 years. A back-of-the-envelope calculation demonstrates the monstrous economic magnitude of this phenomenon. Divorce is, by far, the most powerful re-distributive mechanism in modern society.

Despite recent social advances, women still belong to an economically underprivileged class, are still highly dependent on male patronage and, therefore, are the great beneficiaries of any social, progressive, mechanisms of redistribution. Income taxes, social security, other unilateral transfers, single parent benefits – all accrue mostly to women. The same goes for the "divorce dividend" – the economic windfall profit which is the result of a reasonable and standard divorce.

But economic players are assumed to be rational. Why would a man be a willing party to such an ostensibly disadvantageous arrangement? Who would give up money and assets for no apparent economic benefits? Dividing the matrimonial property in the above mentioned illustrative case is the equivalent of a monthly transfer of US $150 in cash and assets from the husband to his wife throughout their 7 years of marriage.

What is this payment for? Presumably, for services rendered by the woman in-house, in child rearing, as a companion, and in the conjugal bed. This must be the residual value of these services to the man after discounting services that he provides to the woman (including rent for the use of his excess property, sexual services, protection, companionship to the extent that he can provide it, etc.). This is also the marginal value added of these services.

It is safe to say that the value of the services that the woman renders to her man exceed the value of the services that he provides to her – by at least US $150 per month. This excess value accrues to the woman upon divorce.

But this makes only little sense. Consider the woman's ostensible contribution to the couple in the form of children.

Children are an economic liability. They are not revenue generating assets. They do absorb income and convert it to property when they grow up. But the children's property does not belong to the parents. It is outside the ownership, control, and pleasure of both members of the couple.

Every dollar invested by the parents in their offspring's education – is an asset to the off-spring and a liability for the parents. Why should a man stimulate a woman (by providing her with US $150 a month as an incentive) to bring children to the world, raise them, and make them the beneficiaries of the parents' resources?

The couple's offspring compete with their father for scarce resources. It is an economic Oedipus complex. When a woman maintains the house, she preserves its economic value and both members of the couple enjoy it. When she prepares dinner for her mate, or engages in lively talk, or has sex with him – these are services rendered for which the male should be content to pay. But when she raises children –-this both reduces the quality of services that the man can expect to receive from her (by taxing her resources) and diminishes the couple's assets (by transferring them to people outside the marital partnership).

There is only one plausible explanation to this apparently self-defeating economic behavior. Rearing children is an investment with anticipated future rewards (i.e., returns). There is a hidden expectation that this investment will be richly rewarded (i.e., that it will provide reasonable returns).

Indeed, in the not too distant past, children used to support their parents financially, cohabitate with them, or pay for their prolonged stay in convalescence centres and old age homes. Parents regarded their children as the living equivalent of an annuity. "When I grow old" – they would say – "my children will support me and I will not be left alone."

Such an economic arrangement is also common with insurance companies, pension funds and other savings institutions: invest now, reap a monthly cheque in old age. This is the essence of social security. Children were perceived by their parents to be an elaborate form of insurance policy.

Today, things have changed. Higher mobility and the deterioration in familial cohesion rendered this quid pro quo dubious. No parent can rely on future financial support from his children. That would constitute wishful thinking and an imprudent investment policy.

As a result, a rise in the number of divorces is discernible. The existence of children no longer seems to impede or prevent divorces. It seems that, contrary to a widespread misconception, children play no statistically significant role in preserving marriages. People divorce despite their children. And the divorce rate is skyrocketing, as is common knowledge.

The less economically valuable the services rendered by women internally and the more their earning power increases, the more are the monthly transfers from men to women eroded. This looming parity gives impetus to prenuptial property contracts, and to separation of acquests and other forms of matrimonial property.

Women try to keep all their income to themselves and out of the matrimonial property. Men prefer this arrangement as well, because they feel that they are not getting services from women to an extent sufficient to justify a regular monthly transfer. As the economic basis for marriage is corroded – so does the institution of marriage flounder. Marriage is being transformed unrecognizably and assumes an essentially non-economic form, devoid of most of the financial calculations of yore.

Whatever Happened to Sex?

"One is not born, but rather becomes, a woman."

Simone de Beauvoir, The Second Sex (1949)

With same-sex marriage becoming a legal reality throughout the world, many more children are going to be raised by homosexual (gay and lesbian) parents, or even by transgendered or transsexual ones. How is this going to affect the child's masculinity or femininity?

Is being a gay man less manly than being a heterosexual one? Is a woman who is the outcome of a sex change operation less feminine than her natural-born sisters? In which sense is a "virile" lesbian less of a man than an effeminate heterosexual or homosexual man? And how should we classify and treat bisexuals and asexuals?

What about modern she-breadwinners? All those feminist women in traditional male positions who are as sexually aggressive as men and prone to the same varieties of misconduct (e.g., cheating on their spouses)? Are they less womanly? And are their stay-at-home-dad partners not men enough? How are sex preferences related to gender differentiation? And if one's sex and genitalia can be chosen and altered at will – why not one's gender, regardless of one's natural equipment? Can we decouple gender roles from sexual functions and endowments?

Aren't the feminist-liberal-emancipated woman and her responsive, transformed male partner as moulded by specific social norms and narratives as their more traditional and conservative counterparts? And when men adapted to the demands of the "new", post-modernist woman – were they not then rebuffed by that very same female as emasculated and unmanly? What is the source of this gender chaos? Why do people act "modern" while, at heart, they still hark back to erstwhile mores and ethos?

In nature, male and female are distinct. She-elephants are gregarious, he-elephants solitary. Male zebra finches are loquacious - the females mute. Female green spoon worms are 200,000 times larger than their male mates. These striking differences are biological - yet they lead to differentiation in social roles and skill acquisition.

Alan Pease, author of a book titled "Why Men Don't Listen and Women Can't Read Maps", believes that women are spatially-challenged compared to men. The British firm, Admiral Insurance, conducted a study of half a million claims. They found that "women were almost twice as likely as men to have a collision in a car park, 23 percent more likely to hit a stationary car, and 15 percent more likely to reverse into another vehicle" (Reuters).

Yet gender "differences" are often the outcomes of bad scholarship. Consider Admiral Insurance's data. As Britain's Automobile Association (AA) correctly pointed out - women drivers tend to make more short journeys around towns and shopping centers and these involve frequent parking. Hence their ubiquity in certain kinds of claims. Regarding women's alleged spatial deficiency, in Britain, girls have been outperforming boys in scholastic aptitude tests - including geometry and maths - since 1988.

In an Op-Ed published by the New York Times on January 23, 2005, Olivia Judson cited this example

"Beliefs that men are intrinsically better at this or that have repeatedly led to discrimination and prejudice, and then they've been proved to be nonsense. Women were thought not to be world-class musicians. But when American symphony orchestras introduced blind auditions in the 1970's - the musician plays behind a screen so that his or her gender is invisible to those listening - the number of women offered jobs in professional orchestras increased. Similarly, in science, studies of the ways that grant applications are evaluated have shown that women are more likely to get financing when those reading the applications do not know the sex of the applicant."

On the other wing of the divide, Anthony Clare, a British psychiatrist and author of "On Men" wrote:

"At the beginning of the 21st century it is difficult to avoid the conclusion that men are in serious trouble. Throughout the world, developed and developing, antisocial behavior is essentially male. Violence, sexual abuse of children, illicit drug use, alcohol misuse, gambling, all are overwhelmingly male activities. The courts and prisons bulge with men. When it comes to aggression, delinquent behavior, risk taking and social mayhem, men win gold."

Men also mature later, die earlier, are more susceptible to infections and most types of cancer, are more likely to be dyslexic, to suffer from a host of mental health disorders, such as Attention Deficit Hyperactivity Disorder (ADHD), and to commit suicide.

In her book, "Stiffed: The Betrayal of the American Man", Susan Faludi describes a crisis of masculinity following the breakdown of manhood models and work and family structures in the last five decades. In the film "Boys don't Cry", a teenage girl binds her breasts and acts the male in a caricatured relish of stereotypes of virility. Being a man is merely a state of mind, the movie implies.

But what does it really mean to be a "male" or a "female"? Are gender identity and sexual preferences genetically determined? Can they be reduced to one's sex? Or are they amalgams of biological, social, and psychological factors in constant interaction? Are they immutable lifelong features or dynamically evolving frames of self-reference?

In rural northern Albania, until recently, in families with no male heir, women could choose to forego sex and childbearing, alter their external appearance and "become" men and the patriarchs of their clans, with all the attendant rights and obligations.

In the aforementioned New York Times Op-Ed, Olivia Judson opines:

"Many sex differences are not, therefore, the result of his having one gene while she has another. Rather, they are attributable to the way particular genes behave when they find themselves in him instead of her. The magnificent difference between male and female green spoon worms, for example, has nothing to do with their having different genes: each green spoon worm larva could go either way. Which sex it becomes depends on whether it meets a female during its first three weeks of life. If it meets a female, it becomes male and prepares to regurgitate; if it doesn't, it becomes female and settles into a crack on the sea floor."

Yet, certain traits attributed to one's sex are surely better accounted for by the demands of one's environment, by cultural factors, the process of socialization, gender roles, and what George Devereux called "ethnopsychiatry" in "Basic Problems of Ethnopsychiatry" (University of Chicago Press, 1980). He suggested to divide the unconscious into the id (the part that was always instinctual and unconscious) and the "ethnic unconscious" (repressed material that was once conscious). The latter is mostly molded by prevailing cultural mores and includes all our defense mechanisms and most of the superego.

So, how can we tell whether our sexual role is mostly in our blood or in our brains?

The scrutiny of borderline cases of human sexuality - notably the transgendered or intersexed - can yield clues as to the distribution and relative weights of biological, social, and psychological determinants of gender identity formation.

The results of a study conducted by Uwe Hartmann, Hinnerk Becker, and Claudia Rueffer-Hesse in 1997 and titled "Self and Gender: Narcissistic Pathology and Personality Factors in Gender Dysphoric Patients", published in the "International Journal of Transgenderism", "indicate significant psychopathological aspects and narcissistic dysregulation in a substantial proportion of patients." Are these "psychopathological aspects" merely reactions to underlying physiological realities and changes? Could social ostracism and labeling have induced them in the "patients"?

The authors conclude:

"The cumulative evidence of our study ... is consistent with the view that gender dysphoria is a disorder of the sense of self as has been proposed by Beitel (1985) or Pfäfflin (1993). The central problem in our patients is about identity and the self in general and the transsexual wish seems to be an attempt at reassuring and stabilizing the self-coherence which in turn can lead to a further destabilization if the self is already too fragile. In this view the body is instrumentalized to create a sense of identity and the splitting symbolized in the hiatus between the rejected body-self and other parts of the self is more between good and bad objects than between masculine and feminine."

Freud, Kraft-Ebbing, and Fliess suggested that we are all bisexual to a certain degree. As early as 1910, Dr. Magnus Hirschfeld argued, in Berlin, that absolute genders are "abstractions, invented extremes". The consensus today is that one's sexuality is, mostly, a psychological construct which reflects gender role orientation.

Joanne Meyerowitz, a professor of history at Indiana University and the editor of The Journal of American History observes, in her recently published tome, "How Sex Changed: A History of Transsexuality in the United States", that the very meaning of masculinity and femininity is in constant flux.

Transgender activists, says Meyerowitz, insist that gender and sexuality represent "distinct analytical categories". The New York Times wrote in its review of the book: "Some male-to-female transsexuals have sex with men and call themselves homosexuals. Some female-to-male transsexuals have sex with women and call themselves lesbians. Some transsexuals call themselves asexual."

So, it is all in the mind, you see.

This would be taking it too far. A large body of scientific evidence points to the genetic and biological underpinnings of sexual behavior and preferences.

The German science magazine, "Geo", reported recently that the males of the fruit fly "drosophila melanogaster" switched from heterosexuality to homosexuality as the temperature in the lab was increased from 19 to 30 degrees Celsius. They reverted to chasing females as it was lowered.

The brain structures of homosexual sheep are different to those of straight sheep, a study conducted recently by the Oregon Health & Science University and the U.S. Department of Agriculture Sheep Experiment Station in Dubois, Idaho, revealed. Similar differences were found between gay men and straight ones in 1995 in Holland and elsewhere. The preoptic area of the hypothalamus was larger in heterosexual men than in both homosexual men and straight women.

According an article, titled "When Sexual Development Goes Awry", by Suzanne Miller, published in the September 2000 issue of the "World and I", various medical conditions give rise to sexual ambiguity. Congenital adrenal hyperplasia (CAH), involving excessive androgen production by the adrenal cortex, results in mixed genitalia. A person with the complete androgen insensitivity syndrome (AIS) has a vagina, external female genitalia and functioning, androgen-producing, testes - but no uterus or fallopian tubes.

People with the rare 5-alpha reductase deficiency syndrome are born with ambiguous genitalia. They appear at first to be girls. At puberty, such a person develops testicles and his clitoris swells and becomes a penis. Hermaphrodites possess both ovaries and testicles (both, in most cases, rather undeveloped). Sometimes the ovaries and testicles are combined into a chimera called ovotestis.

Most of these individuals have the chromosomal composition of a woman together with traces of the Y, male, chromosome. All hermaphrodites have a sizable penis, though rarely generate sperm. Some hermaphrodites develop breasts during puberty and menstruate. Very few even get pregnant and give birth.

Anne Fausto-Sterling, a developmental geneticist, professor of medical science at Brown University, and author of "Sexing the Body", postulated, in 1993, a continuum of 5 sexes to supplant the current dimorphism: males, merms (male pseudohermaphrodites), herms (true hermaphrodites), ferms (female pseudohermaphrodites), and females.

Intersexuality (hermpahroditism) is a natural human state. We are all conceived with the potential to develop into either sex. The embryonic developmental default is female. A series of triggers during the first weeks of pregnancy places the fetus on the path to maleness.

In rare cases, some women have a male's genetic makeup (XY chromosomes) and vice versa. But, in the vast majority of cases, one of the sexes is clearly selected. Relics of the stifled sex remain, though. Women have the clitoris as a kind of symbolic penis. Men have breasts (mammary glands) and nipples.

The Encyclopedia Britannica 2003 edition describes the formation of ovaries and testes thus:

"In the young embryo a pair of gonads develop that are indifferent or neutral, showing no indication whether they are destined to develop into testes or ovaries. There are also two different duct systems, one of which can develop into the female system of oviducts and related apparatus and the other into the male sperm duct system. As development of the embryo proceeds, either the male or the female reproductive tissue differentiates in the originally neutral gonad of the mammal."

Yet, sexual preferences, genitalia and even secondary sex characteristics, such as facial and pubic hair are first order phenomena. Can genetics and biology account for male and female behavior patterns and social interactions ("gender identity")? Can the multi-tiered complexity and richness of human masculinity and femininity arise from simpler, deterministic, building blocks?

Sociobiologists would have us think so.

For instance: the fact that we are mammals is astonishingly often overlooked. Most mammalian families are composed of mother and offspring. Males are peripatetic absentees. Arguably, high rates of divorce and birth out of wedlock coupled with rising promiscuity merely reinstate this natural "default mode", observes Lionel Tiger, a professor of anthropology at Rutgers University in New Jersey. That three quarters of all divorces are initiated by women tends to support this view.

Furthermore, gender identity is determined during gestation, claim some scholars.

Milton Diamond of the University of Hawaii and Dr. Keith Sigmundson, a practicing psychiatrist, studied the much-celebrated John/Joan case. An accidentally castrated normal male was surgically modified to look female, and raised as a girl but to no avail. He reverted to being a male at puberty.

His gender identity seems to have been inborn (assuming he was not subjected to conflicting cues from his human environment). The case is extensively described in John Colapinto's tome "As Nature Made Him: The Boy Who Was Raised as a Girl".

HealthScoutNews cited a study published in the November 2002 issue of "Child Development". The researchers, from City University of London, found that the level of maternal testosterone during pregnancy affects the behavior of neonatal girls and renders it more masculine. "High testosterone" girls "enjoy activities typically considered male behavior, like playing with trucks or guns". Boys' behavior remains unaltered, according to the study.

Yet, other scholars, like John Money, insist that newborns are a "blank slate" as far as their gender identity is concerned. This is also the prevailing view. Gender and sex-role identities, we are taught, are fully formed in a process of socialization which ends by the third year of life. The Encyclopedia Britannica 2003 edition sums it up thus:

"Like an individual's concept of his or her sex role, gender identity develops by means of parental example, social reinforcement, and language. Parents teach sex-appropriate behavior to their children from an early age, and this behavior is reinforced as the child grows older and enters a wider social world. As the child acquires language, he also learns very early the distinction between "he" and "she" and understands which pertains to him- or herself."

So, which is it - nature or nurture? There is no disputing the fact that our sexual physiology and, in all probability, our sexual preferences are determined in the womb. Men and women are different - physiologically and, as a result, also psychologically.

Society, through its agents - foremost amongst which are family, peers, and teachers - represses or encourages these genetic propensities. It does so by propagating "gender roles" - gender-specific lists of alleged traits, permissible behavior patterns, and prescriptive morals and norms. Our "gender identity" or "sex role" is shorthand for the way we make use of our natural genotypic-phenotypic endowments in conformity with social-cultural "gender roles".

Inevitably as the composition and bias of these lists change, so does the meaning of being "male" or "female". Gender roles are constantly redefined by tectonic shifts in the definition and functioning of basic social units, such as the nuclear family and the workplace. The cross-fertilization of gender-related cultural memes renders "masculinity" and "femininity" fluid concepts.

One's sex equals one's bodily equipment, an objective, finite, and, usually, immutable inventory. But our endowments can be put to many uses, in different cognitive and affective contexts, and subject to varying exegetic frameworks. As opposed to "sex" - "gender" is, therefore, a socio-cultural narrative. Both heterosexual and homosexual men ejaculate. Both straight and lesbian women climax. What distinguishes them from each other are subjective introjects of socio-cultural conventions, not objective, immutable "facts".

In "The New Gender Wars", published in the November/December 2000 issue of "Psychology Today", Sarah Blustain sums up the "bio-social" model proposed by Mice Eagly, a professor of psychology at Northwestern University and a former student of his, Wendy Wood, now a professor at the Texas A&M University:

"Like (the evolutionary psychologists), Eagly and Wood reject social constructionist notions that all gender differences are created by culture. But to the question of where they come from, they answer differently: not our genes but our roles in society. This narrative focuses on how societies respond to the basic biological differences - men's strength and women's reproductive capabilities - and how they encourage men and women to follow certain patterns.

'If you're spending a lot of time nursing your kid', explains Wood, 'then you don't have the opportunity to devote large amounts of time to developing specialized skills and engaging tasks outside of the home'. And, adds Eagly, 'if women are charged with caring for infants, what happens is that women are more nurturing. Societies have to make the adult system work [so] socialization of girls is arranged to give them experience in nurturing'.

According to this interpretation, as the environment changes, so will the range and texture of gender differences. At a time in Western countries when female reproduction is extremely low, nursing is totally optional, childcare alternatives are many, and mechanization lessens the importance of male size and strength, women are no longer restricted as much by their smaller size and by child-bearing. That means, argue Eagly and Wood, that role structures for men and women will change and, not surprisingly, the way we socialize people in these new roles will change too. (Indeed, says Wood, 'sex differences seem to be reduced in societies where men and women have similar status,' she says. If you're looking to live in more gender-neutral environment, try Scandinavia.)"

Film Review: "What to Expect When You Are Expecting" (2012)

Modern pop culture bombards us with gender stereotypes, which by now have become truisms: women are always sensitive, misunderstood, in touch with their emotions and neglected; men are commitment-phobic, confused, narcissistic, hypersexed, and hell-bent on frustrating the opposite number.

It was, therefore, refreshing to watch the four female protagonists of the film "What to Expect When You Are Expecting" reduce these caricatures to smithereens. The womenfolk in the film are self-centered, dread intimacy and commitment, two of them are workaholics, and all four are rank narcissists.

The men in this otherwise middling movie are romantic, in touch with their emotions, committed, and largely selfless. The only exception is the dysfunctional father of one of them, a throwback to the 1960s when men were still machos and sex meant everything. His youthful wife makes up for his shortcomings, though: she is clear-headed, no-nonsense, determined, sharp-witted, and a strict disciplinarian when needed. But this incongruous couple is the only exception to an otherwise coherent message: men have matured, women should get their act together.

The women are the ones who - not so secretly - abhor the thought of what bearing children would do to their bodies and to their lives (in this order.) The men encourage them to be fruitful and multiply as the ultimate fad in self-fulfillment and self-gratification.

Another striking feature of this film is the fact that none of the women, despite being all over the place, feels the need to seek advice. They live alone and cope in solitude: gone are the tips-dispensing mother; the supportive female soulmate; The effeminate or gay male friend; the recurring old flame; the motherly colleague or avuncular co-worker. It's every woman for herself now. And they are botching the job, says the film, as thoroughly as men ever did.

The Death of Traditional Sex in a Unisex World

Traditional sex – the heady cocktail of lust and emotional bonding - is all but dead. In a culture of casual, almost anonymous hookups, suppressing attendant emerging emotions is the bon ton and women and men drift apart, zerovalent atoms in an ever-shifting, kaleidoscopic world, separated by a yawning expectations gap, their virtual isolation aided and abetted by technologies, collectively misnomered "social media".

It is increasingly more difficult to both find a mate and keep him or her. One fifth of all American couples are sexless. In Japan, about half of all adolescents are schizoid and prefer technological gadgets to flesh-and-blood peers. A quarter of all males in Britain would rather watch the telly or bar crawl with their friends than garner carnal pleasure. People everywhere increasingly rely on Internet porn and auto-erotic stimulation to relieve themselves. Sex has become the sordid equivalent of other excretory bodily functions, best pursued in solitude.

At the root of this upheaval is the ill-thought and violent subversion of received gender roles. Women sought to become not only equal to men, but identical to them. Rather than encourage a peaceful evolution, they embarked on a series of shattering and disorienting gender wars with men as the demonized enemy. Attempting assertiveness, women found aggression.

Relationships have become virulent battlefields and the zero testing grounds of a brave, new world. No wonder men find women bafflingly masculine and unattractive. They recoil from commitment and bonding because the rules of engagement are fuzzy, the resources required depleting, the rewards scanty, and the risks – pecuniary and emotional – devastating. Birth rates have plunged well below the replacement rate in most industrialized societies: childrearing requires stable arrangements with reasonable prognoses of functional health and longevity.

In short: the typical, chauvinistic male still wants to get married to his grandmother and his narcissistic female counterparty wishes to live happily ever after with a penile reflection of herself. The differences in expectations lead to discrepancies in performance which are all but unbridgeable and irreconcilable. Breakup rates are unprecedented in human history. The lucrative business of divorce is no longer frowned upon and is facilitated by lenient legislation and a veritable cornucopia of institutions. The proliferation of models of pairing and cohabitation is proof positive that the system is broken: it's every man for himself now. Society is even more clueless and impotent than the individuals it is ostensibly comprised of and, therefore, can provide no normative guidance.

People react to this massive rupture in various ways: some abstain from or renounce sex altogether; a few experiment with bi- or homosexuality; others immerse themselves in cybersex in its multifarious forms; many choose one night stands and random encounters rendered riskless by contraceptives and made widely available via modern transportation and telecommunication. Opportunities for all the above abound and, socially well-tolerated, recreational, non-committal, and emotionless sex is on the rise.

But the roots of the crumbling alliance between men and women go deeper and further in time. Long before divorce became a social norm, men and women grew into two disparate, incompatible, and warring subspecies. Traditionalist, conservative, and religious societies put in place behavioural safeguards against the inevitable wrenching torsion that monogamy entailed: no premarital sex (virginity); no multiple intimate partners; no cohabitation prior to tying the knot; no mobility, or equal rights for women; no mixing of the genders. We now know that each of these habits does, indeed, increase the chances for an ultimate divorce. As Jonathan Franzen elucidates in his literary masterpieces, it boils down to a choice between personal freedoms and the stability of the family: the former decisively preclude the latter.

During the 17th, 18th, and 19th centuries, discreet affairs were an institution of marriage: sexual gratification and emotional intimacy were outsourced while all other domestic functions were shared in partnership. The Industrial Revolution, the Victorian Age, the backlash of the sexual revolution, belligerent feminism, and the advent of socially-atomizing and gender-equalizing transportation, information processing, and telecommunication technologies led inexorably to the hollowing out of family and hearth.

In a civilization centred on brainpower, Men have lost the relative edge that brawn used to provide. Monogamy is increasingly considered as past its expiry date: a historical aberration that reflects the economic and political realities of bygone eras. Moreover: the incidence of lifelong, childfree (or childless) singlehood has skyrocketed as people hope for their potential or actual relationship-partners to provide for all their sexual, emotional, social, and economic needs – and then get sorely disappointed when they fail to meet these highly unrealistic expectations.

In an age of economic self-sufficiency, electronic entertainment, and self-gratification, the art of compromise in relationships is gone. Single motherhood (sometimes via IVF, with no identifiable partner involved) has become the norm in many countries. Even within marriages or committed relationships, solitary pursuits, such as separate vacations, or "girls'/boy' nights out" have become the norm.

The 20th century was a monument to male fatuity: wars and ideologies almost decimated the species. Forced to acquire masculine skills and fill men's shoes in factories and fields, women discovered militant self-autonomy, the superfluousness of men, and the untenability of the male claims to superiority over them.

In an age of malignant individualism, bordering on narcissism, men and women alike put themselves, their fantasies, and their needs first, all else – family included – be damned. And with 5 decades of uninterrupted prosperity, birth control, and feminism/ women's lib most of the female denizens of the West have acquired the financial wherewithal to realize their dreams at the expense and to the detriment of collectives they ostensibly belong to (such as the nuclear family.) Feminism is a movement focused on negatives (obliterating women's age-old bondage) but it offers few constructive ideas regarding women's new roles. By casting men as the enemy, it also failed to educate them and convert them into useful allies.

Owing to the dramatic doubling of life expectancy, modern marriages seem to go through three phases: infatuation (honeymoon); procreation-accumulation (of assets, children, and shared experiences); and exhaustion-outsourcing (bonding with new emotional and sexual partners for rejuvenation or the fulfilment of long-repressed fantasies, needs, and wishes.) Divorces and breakups occur mostly at the seams, the periods of transition between these phases and especially between the stages of accumulation-procreation and exhaustion-outsourcing. This is where family units break down.

With marriage on the decline and infidelity on the rise, the reasonable solution would be swinging (swapping sexual partners) or polyamory (households with multiple partners of both genders all of whom are committed to one another for the long haul, romantically-involved, sexually-shared, and economically united.) Alas, while a perfectly rational development of the traditional marriage and one that is best-suited to modernity, it is an emotionally unstable setup, what with [romantic jealousy](#) ineluctably rearing its ugly head. Very few people are emotionally capable of sharing their life-partner with others.

The question is not why there are so many divorces, but why so few. Surely, serial monogamy is far better, fairer, and more humane than adultery? Couples stay together and tolerate straying owing to inertia; financial or emotional dependence; insecurity (lack of self-confidence or low self-esteem); fear of the unknown and the tedium of dating. Some couples persevere owing to religious conviction of for the sake of appearances. Yet others make a smooth transition to an alternative lifestyle (polyamory, swinging, or consensual adultery).

Indeed, what has changed is not the incidence of adultery, even among women. There are good grounds to assume that it has remained the same throughout human history. The phenomenon - quantitatively and qualitatively - has always been the same, merely underreported. What have changed are the social acceptability of extramarital sex both before and during marriage and the ease of obtaining divorce. People discuss adultery openly where before it was a taboo topic.

Another new development may be the rise of "selfish affairs" among women younger than 35 who are used to multiple sexual partners. "Selfish affairs" are acts of recreational adultery whose sole purpose is to satisfy sexual curiosity and the need for romantic diversity. The emotional component in these usually short-term affairs (one-night stands and the like) is muted. Among women older than 60, adultery has become the accepted way of seeking emotional connection and intimacy outside the marital bond. These are "outsourcing affairs."

The ancient institution of monogamous marriage is ill-suited to the exigencies of modern Western civilization. People of both genders live and [work longer](#) (which renders monogamy impracticable); travel far and away frequently; and are exposed to tempting romantic alternatives via social networking and in various workplace and social settings.

Thus, even as social monogamy and pair commitment and bonding are still largely intact and more condoned than ever and even as infidelity is fervently condemned, sexual exclusivity (mislabelled "sexual monogamy") is declining, especially among the young and the old. Monogamy is becoming one alternative among many lifestyles and marriage only one relationship among a few (sometimes, not even a privileged or unique relationship, as it competes for time and resources with work, same-sex friends, friends with benefits, and opposite-sex friends.)

The contractual aspects of marriage are more pronounced than ever with everything on the table: from extramarital sex (allowed or not) to pre-nuptial agreements. The commodification and preponderance of sex – premarital and extramarital - robbed it of its function as a conduit of specialness and intimacy and since childrearing is largely avoided (natality rates are precipitously plummeting everywhere) or outsourced, the family has lost both its raison d'être and its nature as the venue for exclusive sexual and emotional interactions between adults.

Professed values and prevailing social mores and institutions have yet to catch up to this emerging multifarious reality. The consequences of these discrepancies are disastrous: about 40-50% of all first-time marriages end in divorce and the percentage is much higher for second and third attempts at connubial bliss. Open communication about one's sexual needs is tantamount to self-ruination as one's partner is likely to reflexively initiate a divorce. Dishonesty and cheating are definitely the rational choices in such an unforgiving and punitive environment.

Indeed, most surviving marriages have to do with perpetuating the partners' convenience, their access to commonly-owned assets and future streams of income, and the welfare of third parties, most notably their kids. Erstwhile sexual exclusivity often degenerates into celibacy or abstinence on the one hand – or parallel lives with multiple sexual and emotional partners on the other hand.

One night stands for both genders are usually opportunistic. Extra-pair affairs are self-limiting, as emotional involvement and sexual attraction wane over time. Infidelity is, therefore, much less of a threat to the longevity of a dedicated couple than it is made out to be. Most of the damage is caused by culturally-conditioned, albeit deeply and traumatically felt, reactions to conduct that is almost universally decried as deceitful, dishonest, and in breach of vows and promises.

Until recently, couples formed around promises of emotional exclusivity and sexual fidelity, uniqueness in each other's mind and life, and (more common until the 1940s) virginity. Marriage was also a partnership: economic, or related to childrearing, or companionship. It was based on the partners' past and background and geared towards a shared future.

Nowadays, couples coalesce around the twin undertakings of continuity ("I will ALWAYS be there for you") and availability ("I will always BE there for you.") Issues of exclusivity, uniqueness, and virginity have been relegated to the back-burner. It is no longer practical to demand of one's spouse to have nothing to do with the opposite sex, not to spend the bulk of his or her time outside the marriage, not to take separate vacations, and, more generally, to be joined at the hip. Affairs, for instance – both emotional and sexual – are sad certainties in the life of every couple.

Members of the couple are supposed to make themselves continuously available to each other and to provide emotional sustenance and support in an atmosphere of sharing, companionship, and friendship. All the traditional functions of the family can now be – and often are – outsourced, including even sex and emotional intimacy. But, contrary to marriage, outsourcing is frequently haphazard and unpredictable, dependent as it is on outsiders who are committed elsewhere as well. Hence the relative durability of marriage, in its conservative and less-conventional forms alike: it is a convenient and highly practicable arrangement.

Divorce or other forms of marital breakup are not new phenomena. But their precipitants have undergone a revolutionary shift. In the past, families fell apart owing to a breach of exclusivity, mainly in the forms of emotional or sexual infidelity; a deficiency of uniqueness and primacy: divorced women, for instance, were considered "damaged goods" because they used to "belong" to another man and, therefore, could offer neither primacy nor uniqueness; or an egregious violation of the terms of partnership (for example: sloth, dysfunctional childrearing, infertility).

Nowadays, intimate partners bail out when the continuous availability of their significant others is disrupted: sexually, emotionally, or as friends and companions. Marriages are about the present and are being put to the test on a daily basis. Partners who are dissatisfied opt out and team up with other, more promising providers. Children are serially reared by multiple parents and in multiple households.

The Lifestyle (Swinging)

Click HERE to Watch the Video

The Lifestyle involves sexual acts performed by more than two participants whether in the same space, or separately. It is also known as "swinging", "wife-, or spouse-swapping", "wife-, or spouse-sharing", "group sex" and, where multiple people interact with a single person, "gangbanging". Swinging can be soft (engaging in sexual activity with one's own intimate partner, but in the presence of others), or hard (having sex not with one's spouse or mate.) Threesomes (mostly male-female-male or MFM) are the most common configuration.

The psychological background to such unusual pursuits is not clear and has never been studied in depth. Still, thousands of online chats between active and wannabe adherents and fans in various forums reveal 10 psychodynamic strands:

1. Latent and overt **bisexuality and homosexuality**: both men and women (but especially women) adopt swinging as a way to sample same-sex experiences in a tolerant, at times anonymous, and permissive environment;

2. The **Slut-Madonna Complex**: to be sexually attracted to their spouses, some men need to "debase" and "humiliate" them by witnessing their "sluttish" conduct with others. These men find it difficult to have regular, intimate sex with women to whom they are emotionally attached and whose probity is beyond doubt. Sex is "dirty" and demeaning, so it should be mechanical, the preserve of whorish and promiscuous partners;

3. **Voyeurism and exhibitionism** are both rampant in and satisfied by swinging. Oftentimes, those who partake in the Lifestyle document their exploits on video and share photos and saucy verbal descriptions. Amateur porn and public sex ("dogging") are fixtures of swinging;

4. **Vicarious gratification.** "Cuckolds" are (typically male) swingers who masturbate to the sight of their partner having sex with another, usually without actually joining the fray. They derive gratification from and are sexually aroused by the evident pleasure experienced by their significant other: her vocalizations, body language, body fluids, enraptured movements, and orgasm and abandon;

5. **Masochism** is a prime motive for a minority of swingers. They relish in their own agony as they watch their spouse hooking up with others: envy, pain, anxiety, a sense of humiliation, an overpowering feeling of worthlessness and inadequacy, sinfulness, debauchery, depravity, and decadence all conspire to thrill the masochist and delight him;

6. Swinging is also a form of **legitimized cheating**. It spices up the stale sex lives of the players and neutralized the emotional and financial risks and threats associated with furtive extramarital escapades. Many swingers adopt the Lifestyle in order to alleviate boredom, counter routine, realise sexual fantasies, learn new techniques, feel desirable and attractive once more, and cope with discrepancies in sex drive. They insist: "swinging saved my marriage";

7. Some swingers use the Lifestyle to "display" or "exhibit" their partners, casting them as desired and desirable **trophies**, or **status symbols**. Others present may sexually "sample the wife" but never own her, a form of restricted access which causes her suitors much envy and frustration. "I am the one who ends up going home with her" – these swingers brag, thus reaffirming their own irresistibility and attractiveness;

8. The Lifestyle is a rollercoaster of serial relationships, mostly with strangers. It is, therefore, thrilling, risky, and exciting and provokes anxiety, romantic jealousy, and guilt (for having dragged the partner into the Lifestyle, or for not having restrained her). There is also a recurrent fear of losing the partner owing to a growing emotional or sexual bond with one of her casual "F-buddies" or "friends with benefits". Swinging results in an **adrenaline rush**, a high, and in addictive periods of calm after these self-inflicted psychosexual storms;

9. Swinging calls for the **objectification** of sexual partners. Many swingers prefer to remain anonymous in settings like Lifestyle retreats or group sex and orgies. They are thus reduced to genitalia and erogenous zones enmeshed in auto-erotic and narcissistic acts of masturbatory gratification with other people's bodies as mere props. Women reported experiencing a new sense of empowerment and mastery as they can finally dictate the terms and conditions of sexual encounters, pick and choose partners, and realize hitherto suppressed sexual fantasies. Other practitioners actually prefer to swing only with close friends, using sex as a form of intimacy-enhancing **recreation**;

10. Nudity has a pronounced **aesthetic dimension** and when multiple naked bodies intertwine, the combination can amount to a work of art, a flesh-and-blood throbbing sculpture. Many swingers find sex to be the most supreme form of artistic experience, an interconnectedness that enhances empathy and communication and provides extreme sensual pleasure. It is also great fun: the ultimate in entertainment, where novelty and familiarity merge to yield a unique journey with each new entrant.

Homosexuality: The Natural Roots of Sexuality

Recent studies in animal sexuality serve to dispel two common myths: that sex is exclusively about reproduction and that homosexuality is an unnatural sexual preference. It now appears that sex is also about recreation as it frequently occurs out of the mating season. And same-sex copulation and bonding are common in hundreds of species, from bonobo apes to gulls.

Moreover, homosexual couples in the Animal Kingdom are prone to behaviors commonly - and erroneously - attributed only to heterosexuals. The New York Times reported in its February 7, 2004 issue about a couple of gay penguins who are desperately and recurrently seeking to incubate eggs together.

In the same article ("Love that Dare not Squeak its Name"), Bruce Bagemihl, author of the groundbreaking *"Biological Exuberance: Animal Homosexuality and Natural Diversity"*, defines homosexuality as *"any of these behaviors between members of the same sex: long-term bonding, sexual contact, courtship displays or the rearing of young."*

Still, that a certain behavior occurs in nature (is "natural") does not render it moral. Infanticide, patricide, suicide, gender bias, and substance abuse - are all to be found in various animal species. It is futile to argue for homosexuality or against it based on zoological observations. Ethics is about surpassing nature - not about emulating it.

The more perplexing question remains: what are the evolutionary and biological advantages of recreational sex and homosexuality? Surely, both entail the waste of scarce resources.

Convoluted explanations, such as the one proffered by Marlene Zuk (homosexuals contribute to the gene pool by nurturing and raising young relatives) defy common sense, experience, and the calculus of evolution. There are no field studies that show conclusively or even indicate that homosexuals tend to raise and nurture their younger relatives more that straights do.

Moreover, the arithmetic of genetics would rule out such a stratagem. If the aim of life is to pass on one's genes from one generation to the next, the homosexual would have been far better off raising his own children (who carry forward half his DNA) - rather than his nephew or niece (with whom he shares merely one quarter of his genetic material.)

What is more, though genetically-predisposed, homosexuality may be partly acquired, the outcome of environment and nurture, rather than nature.

An oft-overlooked fact is that recreational sex and homosexuality have one thing in common: they do not lead to reproduction. Homosexuality may, therefore, be a form of pleasurable sexual play. It may also enhance same-sex bonding and train the young to form cohesive, purposeful groups (the army and the boarding school come to mind).

Furthermore, homosexuality amounts to the culling of 10-15% of the gene pool in each generation. The genetic material of the homosexual is not propagated and is effectively excluded from the big roulette of life. Growers - of anything from cereals to cattle - similarly use random culling to improve their stock. As mathematical models show, such repeated mass removal of DNA from the common brew seems to optimize the species and increase its resilience and efficiency.

It is ironic to realize that homosexuality and other forms of non-reproductive, pleasure-seeking sex may be key evolutionary mechanisms and integral drivers of population dynamics. Reproduction is but one goal among many, equally important, end results. Heterosexuality is but one strategy among a few optimal solutions. Studying biology may yet lead to greater tolerance for the vast repertoire of human sexual foibles, preferences, and predilections. Back to nature, in this case, may be forward to civilization.

Suggested Literature

Bagemihl, Bruce - ***"Biological Exuberance: Animal Homosexuality and Natural Diversity"*** - St. Martin's Press, 1999

De-Waal, Frans and Lanting, Frans - ***"Bonobo: The Forgotten Ape"*** - University of California Press, 1997

De Waal, Frans - ***"Bonobo Sex and Society"*** - March 1995 issue of Scientific American, pp. 82-88

Trivers, Robert - *Natural Selection and Social Theory: Selected Papers* - Oxford University Press, 2002

Zuk, Marlene - ***"Sexual Selections: What We Can and Can't Learn About Sex From Animals"*** - University of California Press, 2002

Parenting: The Irrational Vocation

The advent of cloning, surrogate motherhood, and the donation of gametes and sperm have shaken the traditional biological definition of parenthood to its foundations. The social roles of parents have similarly been recast by the decline of the nuclear family and the surge of alternative household formats.

Why do people become parents in the first place? Do we have a moral obligation to humanity at large, to ourselves, or to our unborn children? Hardly.

Raising children comprises equal measures of satisfaction and frustration. Parents often employ a psychological defense mechanism - known as "cognitive dissonance" - to suppress the negative aspects of parenting and to deny the unpalatable fact that raising children is time consuming, exhausting, and strains otherwise pleasurable and tranquil relationships to their limits.

Not to mention the fact that the gestational mother experiences *"considerable discomfort, effort, and risk in the course of pregnancy and childbirth"* (Narayan, U., and J.J. Bartkowiak (1999) **Having and Raising Children: Unconventional Families, Hard Choices, and the Social Good** University Park, PA: The Pennsylvania State University Press, Quoted in the Stanford Encyclopedia of Philosophy).

Parenting is possibly an irrational vocation, but humanity keeps breeding and procreating. It may well be the call of nature. All living species reproduce and most of them parent. Is maternity (and paternity) proof that, beneath the ephemeral veneer of civilization, we are still merely a kind of beast, subject to the impulses and hard-wired behavior that permeate the rest of the animal kingdom?

In his seminal tome, **"The Selfish Gene"**, Richard Dawkins suggested that we copulate in order to preserve our genetic material by embedding it in the future gene pool. Survival itself - whether in the form of DNA, or, on a higher-level, as a species - determines our parenting instinct. Breeding and nurturing the young are mere safe conduct mechanisms, handing the precious cargo of genetics down generations of "organic containers".

Yet, surely, to ignore the epistemological and emotional realities of parenthood is misleadingly reductionistic. Moreover, Dawkins commits the scientific faux-pas of teleology. Nature has no purpose "in mind", mainly because it has no mind. Things simply are, period. That genes end up being forwarded in time does not entail that Nature (or, for that matter, "God") planned it this way. Arguments from design have long - and convincingly - been refuted by countless philosophers.

Still, human beings do act intentionally. Back to square one: why bring children to the world and burden ourselves with decades of commitment to perfect strangers?

First hypothesis: offspring allow us to "delay" death. Our progeny are the medium through which our genetic material is propagated and immortalized. Additionally, by remembering us, our children "keep us alive" after physical death.

These, of course, are self-delusional, self-serving, illusions.

Our genetic material gets diluted with time. While it constitutes 50% of the first generation - it amounts to a measly 6% three generations later. If the everlastingness of one's unadulterated DNA was the paramount concern – incest would have been the norm.

As for one's enduring memory - well, do you recall or can you name your maternal or paternal great great grandfather? Of course you can't. So much for that. Intellectual feats or architectural monuments are far more potent mementos.

Still, we have been so well-indoctrinated that this misconception - that children equal immortality - yields a baby boom in each post war period. Having been existentially threatened, people multiply in the vain belief that they thus best protect their genetic heritage and their memory.

Let's study another explanation.

The utilitarian view is that one's offspring are an asset - kind of pension plan and insurance policy rolled into one. Children are still treated as a yielding property in many parts of the world. They plough fields and do menial jobs very effectively. People "hedge their bets" by bringing multiple copies of themselves to the world. Indeed, as infant mortality plunges - in the better-educated, higher income parts of the world - so does fecundity.

In the Western world, though, children have long ceased to be a profitable proposition. At present, they are more of an economic drag and a liability. Many continue to live with their parents into their thirties and consume the family's savings in college tuition, sumptuous weddings, expensive divorces, and parasitic habits. Alternatively, increasing mobility breaks families apart at an early stage. Either way, children are not longer the founts of emotional sustenance and monetary support they allegedly used to be.

How about this one then:

Procreation serves to preserve the cohesiveness of the family nucleus. It further bonds father to mother and strengthens the ties between siblings. Or is it the other way around and a cohesive and warm family is conductive to reproduction?

Both statements, alas, are false.

Stable and functional families sport far fewer children than abnormal or dysfunctional ones. Between one third and one half of all children are born in single parent or in other non-traditional, non-nuclear - typically poor and under-educated - households. In such families children are mostly born unwanted and unwelcome - the sad outcomes of accidents and mishaps, wrong fertility planning, lust gone awry and misguided turns of events.

The more sexually active people are and the less safe their desirous exploits – the more they are likely to end up with a bundle of joy (the American saccharine expression for a newborn). Many children are the results of sexual ignorance, bad timing, and a vigorous and undisciplined sexual drive among teenagers, the poor, and the less educated.

Still, there is no denying that most people want their kids and love them. They are attached to them and experience grief and bereavement when they die, depart, or are sick. Most parents find parenthood emotionally fulfilling, happiness-inducing, and highly satisfying. This pertains even to unplanned and initially unwanted new arrivals.

Could this be the missing link? Do fatherhood and motherhood revolve around self-gratification? Does it all boil down to the pleasure principle?

Childrearing may, indeed, be habit forming. Nine months of pregnancy and a host of social positive reinforcements and expectations condition the parents to do the job. Still, a living tot is nothing like the abstract concept. Babies cry, soil themselves and their environment, stink, and severely disrupt the lives of their parents. Nothing too enticing here.

One's spawns are a risky venture. So many things can and do go wrong. So few expectations, wishes, and dreams are realized. So much pain is inflicted on the parents. And then the child runs off and his procreators are left to face the "empty nest". The emotional "returns" on a child are rarely commensurate with the magnitude of the investment.

If you eliminate the impossible, what is left - however improbable - must be the truth. People multiply because it provides them with narcissistic supply.

A Narcissist is a person who projects a (false) image unto others and uses the interest this generates to regulate a labile and grandiose sense of self-worth. The reactions garnered by the narcissist - attention, unconditional acceptance, adulation, admiration, affirmation - are collectively known as "narcissistic supply". The narcissist objectifies people and treats them as mere instruments of gratification.

Infants go through a phase of unbridled fantasy, tyrannical behavior, and perceived omnipotence. An adult narcissist, in other words, is still stuck in his "terrible twos" and is possessed with the emotional maturity of a toddler. To some degree, we are all narcissists. Yet, as we grow, we learn to empathize and to love ourselves and others.

This edifice of maturity is severely tested by newfound parenthood.

Babies evokes in the parent the most primordial drives, protective, animalistic instincts, the desire to merge with the newborn and a sense of terror generated by such a desire (a fear of vanishing and of being assimilated). Neonates engender in their parents an emotional regression.

The parents find themselves revisiting their own childhood even as they are caring for the newborn. The crumbling of decades and layers of personal growth is accompanied by a resurgence of the aforementioned early infancy narcissistic defenses. Parents - especially new ones - are gradually transformed into narcissists by this encounter and find in their children the perfect sources of narcissistic supply, euphemistically known as love. Really it is a form of symbiotic codependence of both parties.

Even the most balanced, most mature, most psychodynamically stable of parents finds such a flood of narcissistic supply irresistible and addictive. It enhances his or her self-confidence, buttresses self esteem, regulates the sense of self-worth, and projects a complimentary image of the parent to himself or herself.

It fast becomes indispensable, especially in the emotionally vulnerable position in which the parent finds herself, with the reawakening and repetition of all the unresolved conflicts that she had with her own parents.

If this theory is true, if breeding is merely about securing prime quality narcissistic supply, then the higher the self confidence, the self esteem, the self worth of the parent, the clearer and more realistic his self image, and the more abundant his other sources of narcissistic supply - the fewer children he will have. These predictions are borne out by reality.

The higher the education and the income of adults – and, consequently, the firmer their sense of self worth - the fewer children they have. Children are perceived as counter-productive: not only is their output (narcissistic supply) redundant, they hinder the parent's professional and pecuniary progress.

The more children people can economically afford – the fewer they have. This gives the lie to the Selfish Gene hypothesis. The more educated they are, the more they know about the world and about themselves, the less they seek to procreate. The more advanced the civilization, the more efforts it invests in preventing the birth of children. Contraceptives, family planning, and abortions are typical of affluent, well informed societies.

The more plentiful the narcissistic supply afforded by other sources – the lesser the emphasis on breeding. Freud described the mechanism of sublimation: the sex drive, the Eros (libido), can be "converted", "sublimated" into other activities. All the sublimatory channels - politics and art, for instance - are narcissistic and yield narcissistic supply. They render children superfluous. Creative people have fewer children than the average or none at all. This is because they are narcissistically self sufficient.

The key to our determination to have children is our wish to experience the same unconditional love that we received from our mothers, this intoxicating feeling of being adored without caveats, for what we are, with no limits, reservations, or calculations. This is the most powerful, crystallized form of narcissistic supply. It nourishes our self-love, self worth and self-confidence. It infuses us with feelings of omnipotence and omniscience. In these, and other respects, parenthood is a return to infancy.

Note: Parenting as a Moral Obligation

Do we have a moral obligation to become parents? Some would say: yes. There are three types of arguments to support such a contention:

(i) We owe it to humanity at large to propagate the species or to society to provide manpower for future tasks

(ii) We owe it to ourselves to realize our full potential as human beings and as males or females by becoming parents

(iii) We owe it to our unborn children to give them life.

The first two arguments are easy to dispense with. We have a minimal moral obligation to humanity and society and that is to conduct ourselves so as not to harm others. All other ethical edicts are either derivative or spurious. Similarly, we have a minimal moral obligation to ourselves and that is to be happy (while not harming others). If bringing children to the world makes us happy, all for the better. If we would rather not procreate, it is perfectly within our rights not to do so.

But what about the third argument?

Only living people have rights. There is a debate whether an egg is a living person, but there can be no doubt that it exists. Its rights - whatever they are - derive from the fact that it exists and that it has the potential to develop life. The right to be brought to life (the right to become or to be) pertains to a yet non-alive entity and, therefore, is null and void. Had this right existed, it would have implied an obligation or duty to give life to the unborn and the not yet conceived. No such duty or obligation exist.

"Parasite singles", "boomerang kids", and "accordion families"

"One man cannot be a warrior on a battlefield."
(Russian proverb)

The Japanese call them "parasite singles", the Americans "boomerang kids". Sociologists refer to the "accordion family": it expands and then contracts as children return to what should have been an "empty nest." With an anemic jobs market (youth unemployment hovers above 20% throughout the industrial world), extended education, and a culture of rampant individualism (not to say egotistical narcissism), parents are forced to continue to bankroll their children and take care of their needs well into their offspring's thirties. Infantilism rocks and rules.

There is no word for it in Russian. Platon Karatayev, the typical "Russian soul" in Tolstoy's "War and Peace", extols, for pages at a time, the virtues of communality and disparages the individual - this otherwise useless part of the greater whole. In Macedonia the words "private" or "privacy" pertain to matters economic. The word "intimacy" is used instead to designate the state of being free of prying, intrusive eyes and acts of meddling. Throughout Central and Eastern Europe, the rise of "individualism" did not give birth to its corollary: "privacy". After decades (and, in most cases, centuries) of cramped, multi-generational shared accommodation, it is no wonder.

To the alienated and schizoid ears of Westerners, the survival of family and community in CEE sounds like an attractive proposition. A dual purpose safety net, both emotional and economic, the family in countries in transition provides its members with unemployment benefits, accommodation, food and psychological advice to boot. Divorced daughters, saddled with little (and not so little) ones, the prodigal sons incapable of finding a job befitting their qualifications, the sick, the unhappy - all are absorbed by the compassionate bosom of the family and, by extension the community. The family, the neighbourhood, the community, the village, the tribe - are units of subversion as well as useful safety valves, releasing and regulating the pressures of contemporary life in the modern, materialistic, crime ridden state. The ancient blood feud laws of the kanoon were handed over through familial lineages in northern Albania, in defiance of the paranoiac Enver Hoxha regime. Criminals hide among their kin in the Balkans, thus effectively evading the long arm of the law (state). Jobs are granted, contracts signed and tenders won on an open and strict nepotistic basis and no one finds it odd or wrong. There is something atavistically heart-warming in all this.

Historically, the rural units of socialization and social organization were the family and the village. As villagers migrated to the cities, these structural and functional patterns were imported by them, en masse. The shortage of urban apartments and the communist invention of the communal apartment (its tiny rooms allocated one per family with kitchen and bathroom common to all) only served to perpetuate these ancient modes of multi-generational huddling. At best, the few available apartments were shared by three generations: parents, married off-spring and their children. In many cases, the living space was also shared by sickly or no-good relatives and even by unrelated families.

These living arrangements - more adapted to rustic open spaces than to high rises - led to severe social and psychological dysfunctions. To this very day, Balkan males are spoiled by the subservience and servitude of their in-house parents and incessantly and compulsively catered to by their submissive wives. Occupying someone else's home, they are not well acquainted with adult responsibilities. Stunted growth and stagnant immaturity are the hallmarks of an entire generation, stifled by the ominous proximity of suffocating, invasive love. Unable to lead a healthy sex life behind paper thin walls, unable to raise their children and as many children as they see fit, unable to develop emotionally under the anxiously watchful eye of their parents - this greenhouse generation is doomed to a zombie-like existence in the twilight nether land of their parents' caves. Many ever more eagerly await the demise of their caring captors and the promised land of their inherited apartments, free of their parents' presence.

The daily pressures and exigencies of co-existence are enormous. The prying, the gossip, the criticism, the chastising, the small agitating mannerisms, the smells, the incompatible personal habits and preferences, the pusillanimous bookkeeping - all serve to erode the individual and to reduce him or her to the most primitive mode of survival. This is further exacerbated by the need to share expenses, to allocate labour and tasks, to plan ahead for contingencies, to see off threats, to hide information, to pretend and to fend off emotionally injurious behaviour. It is a sweltering tropic of affective cancer.

Newly found materialism brought these territories a malignant form of capitalism coupled with a sub-culture of drugs and crime. The eventuating disintegration of all polities in the ensuing moral vacuum was complete. From the more complex federations or states and their governments, through intermediate municipalities and down to the most primitive of political cells - the family - they all crumbled in a storm of discontent and blood. The mutant frontier-"independence" or pioneer-"individualism" imported from Western B movies led to a functional upheaval unmatched by a structural one. People want privacy and intimacy more than ever - but they still inhabit the same shoddily constructed, congested accommodation and they still earn poorly or are unemployed. This tension between aspiration and perspiration is potentially revolutionary. It is this unaccomplished, uneasy metamorphosis that tore the social fabric of CEE apart, rendering it poisoned and dysfunctional. This is nothing new - it is what brought socialism and its more vicious variants down.

But what is new is inequality. Ever the pathologically envious, the citizens of CEE bathed in common misery. The equal distribution of poverty and hardship guaranteed their peace of mind. A Jewish proverb says: "the trouble of the many is half a consolation". It is this breakdown of symmetry of wretchedness that really shook the social order. The privacy and intimacy and freedom gained by the few are bound to incite the many into acts of desperation. After all, what can be more individualistic, more private, more mind requiting, more tranquillizing than being part of a riotous mob intent of implementing a platform of hate and devastation?

The Virtual Home

On June 9, 2005 the BBC reported about an unusual project underway in Sheffield (in the United Kingdom). The daily movements and interactions of a family living in a technology-laden, futuristic home are being monitored and recorded. "The aim is to help house builders predict how we will want to use our homes 10 or 20 years from now." - explained the reporter.

The home of the future may be quite a chilling - or uplifting - prospect, depending on one's prejudices and predilections.

Christopher Sanderson, of The Future Laboratory and Richard Brindley, of the Royal Institute of British Architects describe smaller flats with movable walls as a probable response to over-crowding. Home systems will cater to all the entertainment and media needs of the inhabitants further insulating them from their social milieu.

Even hobbies will move indoors. Almost every avocation - from cooking to hiking - can now be indulged at home with pro-am (professional-amateur) equipment. We may become self-sufficient as far as functions we now outsource - such as education and dry cleaning - go. Lastly, in the long-run, robots are likely to replace some pets and many human interactions.

These technological developments will have grave effects on family cohesion and functioning.

The family is the mainspring of support of every kind. It mobilizes psychological resources and alleviates emotional burdens. It allows for the sharing of tasks, provides material goods together with cognitive training. It is the prime socialization agent and encourages the absorption of information, most of it useful and adaptive.

This division of labour between parents and children is vital both to development and to proper adaptation. The child must feel, in a functional family, that s/he can share his experiences without being defensive and that the feedback that s/he is likely to receive will be open and unbiased. The only "bias" acceptable (because it is consistent with constant outside feedback) is the set of beliefs, values and goals that is internalized via imitation and unconscious identification.

So, the family is the first and the most important source of identity and of emotional support. It is a greenhouse wherein a child feels loved, accepted and secure - the prerequisites for the development of personal resources. On the material level, the family should provide the basic necessities (and, preferably, beyond), physical care and protection and refuge and shelter during crises.

Elsewhere, we have discussed the role of the mother (The Primary Object). The father's part is mostly neglected, even in professional literature. However, recent research demonstrates his importance to the orderly and healthy development of the child.

He participates in the day to day care, is an intellectual catalyst, who encourages the child to develop his interests and to satisfy his curiosity through the manipulation of various instruments and games. He is a source of authority and discipline, a boundary setter, enforcing and encouraging positive behaviors and eliminating negative ones. He also provides emotional support and economic security, thus stabilizing the family unit. Finally, he is the prime source of masculine orientation and identification to the male child - and gives warmth and love as a male to his daughter, without exceeding the socially permissible limits.

These traditional roles of the family are being eroded from both the inside and the outside. The proper functioning of the classical family was determined, to a large extent, by the geographical proximity of its members. They all huddled together in the "family unit" – an identifiable volume of physical space, distinct and different to other units. The daily friction and interaction between the members of the family molded them, influenced their patterns of behavior and their reactive patterns and determined how successful their adaptation to life would be.

With the introduction of modern, fast transportation and telecommunications, it was no longer possible to confine the members of the family to the household, to the village, or even to the neighborhood. The industrial revolution splintered the classical family and scattered its members.

Still, the result was not the disappearance of the family but the formation of nuclear families: leaner and meaner units of production. The extended family of yore (three or four generations) merely spread its wings over a greater physical distance – but in principle, remained almost intact.

Grandma and grandpa would live in one city with a few of the younger or less successful aunts and uncles. Their other daughters or sons would be married and moved to live either in another part of the same city, or in another geographical location (even in another continent). But contact was maintained by more or less frequent visits, reunions and meetings on opportune or critical occasions.

This was true well into the 1950s.

However, a series of developments in the second half of the twentieth century threatens to completely decouple the family from its physical dimension. We are in the process of experimenting with the family of the future: the virtual family. This is a family devoid of any spatial (geographical) or temporal identity. Its members do not necessarily share the same genetic heritage (the same blood lineage). It is bound mainly by communication, rather than by interests. Its domicile is cyberspace, its residence in the realm of the symbolic.

Urbanization and industrialization pulverized the structure of the family, by placing it under enormous pressures and by causing it to relegate most of its functions to outside agencies: education was taken over by schools, health – by (national or private) health plans, entertainment by television, interpersonal communication by telephony and computers, socialization by the mass media and the school system and so on.

Devoid of its traditional functions, subject to torsion and other elastic forces – the family was torn apart and gradually stripped of its meaning. The main functions left to the family unit were the provision of the comfort of familiarity (shelter) and serving as a physical venue for leisure activities.

The first role - familiarity, comfort, security, and shelter - was eroded by the global brands.

The "Home Away from Home" business concept means that multinational brands such as Coca-Cola and McDonalds foster familiarity where previously there was none. Needless to say that the etymological closeness between "family" and "familiar" is no accident. The estrangement felt by foreigners in a foreign land is, thus, alleviated, as the world is fast becoming mono-cultural.

The "Family of Man" and the "Global Village" have replaced the nuclear family and the physical, historic, village. A businessman feels more at home in any Sheraton or Hilton than in the living room of his ageing parents. An academician feels more comfortable in any faculty in any university than with his own nuclear or immediate family. One's old neighborhood is a source of embarrassment rather than a fount of strength.

The family's second function - leisure activities - fell prey to the advance of the internet and digital and wireless telecommunications.

Whereas the hallmark of the classical family was that it had clear spatial and temporal coordinates – the virtual family has none. Its members can (and often do) live in different continents. They communicate by digital means. They have electronic mail (rather than the physical post office box). They have a "HOME page". They have a "webSITE".

In other words, they have the virtual equivalents of geographical reality, a "VIRTUAL reality" or "virtual existence". In the not so distant future, people will visit each other electronically and sophisticated cameras will allow them to do so in three-dimensional format.

The temporal dimension, which was hitherto indispensable in human interactions – being at the same place in the same time in order to interact - is also becoming unnecessary. Voicemail and videomail messages will be left in electronic "boxes" to be retrieved at the convenience of the recipient. Meetings in person will be made redundant with the advent of video-conferencing.

The family will not remain unaffected. A clear distinction will emerge between the biological family and the virtual family. A person will be born into the first but will regard this fact as accidental. Blood relations will count less than virtual relations. Individual growth will involve the formation of a virtual family, as well as a biological one (getting married and having children). People will feel equally at ease anywhere in the world for two reasons:

1. There will be no appreciable or discernible difference between geographical locations. Separate will no longer mean disparate. A McDonald's and a Coca-Cola and a Hollywood produced movie are already available everywhere and always. So will the internet treasures of knowledge and entertainment.

2. Interactions with the outside world will be minimized. People will conduct their lives more and more indoors. They will communicate with others (their biological original family included) via telecommunications devices and the internet. They will spend most of their time, work and create in the cyber-world. Their true (really, only) home will be their website. Their only reliably permanent address will be their e-mail address. Their enduring friendships will be with co-chatters. They will work from home, flexibly and independently of others. They will customize their cultural consumption using 500 channel televisions based on video on demand technology.

Hermetic and mutually exclusive universes will be the end result of this process. People will be linked by very few common experiences within the framework of virtual communities. They will haul their world with them as they move about. The miniaturization of storage devices will permit them to carry whole libraries of data and entertainment in their suitcase or backpack or pocket.

It is true that all these predictions are extrapolations of technological breakthroughs and devices, which are in their embryonic stages and are limited to affluent, English-speaking, societies in the West. But the trends are clear and they mean ever-increasing differentiation, isolation and individuation. This is the last assault, which the family will not survive. Already most households consist of "irregular" families (single parents, same sex, etc.). The rise of the virtual family will sweep even these transitory forms aside.

Social Costs of Small Business

Big Business (with 1000 employees or more) and traditional business (central office or factory) provided workers with a network of social contacts and with opportunities to fraternize and befriend others. These workplaces fostered the formation of formal and informal emotional and economic peer-based support groups. These benefits were lost with the advent of the Small Office Home Office (SOHO), flextime, and personal entrepreneurship.

Tens of millions started to work from home, acting as subcontractors for larger corporations and using telecommunications technology (most recently the Internet, laptops, smartphones, and enterprise collaboration software). Transformed by these technological and social upheavals, even Big Business now consists of virtual (cyber), ad-hoc, self-assembling, largely non-hierarchical collaborative webs.

The result is the atomization of the workforce. People rarely see or meet each other in the flesh. No amount of teambuilding, get-togethers, and enterprise social networking can make up for this loss of personal touch and the loneliness and sense of drift that it engenders. Normally, this isolation has had an effect on the work ethic (somewhat negative), productivity (largely positive), and loyalty (very negative.)

Interview granted to <u>Women's International Perspective</u>:

Do you think our social bonds are at a breaking point because of an influx of electronics? Do you think the pervasiveness of technology has lead to increased isolation? How?

Technology had and has a devastating effect on the survival and functioning of core social units, such as the community/neighborhood and, most crucially, the family.

With the introduction of modern, fast transportation and telecommunications, it was no longer possible to confine the members of the family to the household, to the village, or even to the neighborhood. The industrial and, later information revolutions splintered the classical family and scattered its members as they outsourced the family's functions (such as feeding, education, and entertainment).

This process is on-going: interactions with the outside world are being minimized. People conduct their lives more and more indoors. They communicate with others (their biological original family included) via telecommunications devices and the internet. They spend most of their time, work and create in the cyber-world. Their true (really, only) home is their website or page on the social network du jour. Their only reliably permanent address is their e-mail address. Their enduring albeit ersatz friendships are with co-chatters. They work from home, flexibly and independently of others. They customize their cultural consumption using 500 channel televisions based on video on demand technology.

Hermetic and mutually exclusive universes will be the end result of this process. People will be linked by very few common experiences within the framework of virtual communities. They will haul their world with them as they move about. The miniaturization of storage devices will permit them to carry whole libraries of data and entertainment in their suitcase or backpack or pocket. They will no longer need or resort to physical interactions.

Why is it important for humans to 'reach out and touch' fellow human beings?

Modern technology allows us to reach out, but rarely to truly touch. It substitutes kaleidoscopic, brief, and shallow interactions for long, meaningful and deep relationships. Our abilities to empathize and to collaborate with each other are like muscles: they require frequent exercise. Gradually, we are being denied the opportunity to flex them and, thus, we empathize less; we collaborate more fitfully and inefficiently; we act more narcissistically and antisocially. Functioning society is rendered atomized and anomic by technology.

II. The Pathological

The Pathology of Love

The unpalatable truth is that falling in love is, in some ways, indistinguishable from a severe pathology. Behavior changes are reminiscent of psychosis and, biochemically speaking, passionate love closely imitates substance abuse. Appearing in the BBC series Body Hits on December 4, 2002 Dr. John Marsden, the head of the British National Addiction Center, said that love is addictive, akin to cocaine and speed. Sex is a "booby trap", intended to bind the partners long enough to bond.

Using functional Magnetic Resonance Imaging (fMRI), Andreas Bartels and Semir Zeki of University College in London showed that the same areas of the brain are active when abusing drugs and when in love. The prefrontal cortex - hyperactive in depressed patients - is inactive when besotted. How can this be reconciled with the low levels of serotonin that are the telltale sign of both depression and infatuation - is not known.

Other MRI studies, conducted in 2006-7 by Dr. Lucy Brown, a professor in the department of neurology and neuroscience at the Albert Einstein College of Medicine in New York, and her colleagues, revealed that the caudate and the ventral tegmental, brain areas involved in cravings (e.g., for food) and the secretion of dopamine, are lit up in subjects who view photos of their loved ones. Dopamine is a neurotransmitter that affects pleasure and motivation. It causes a sensation akin to a substance-induced high.

On August 14, 2007, the New Scientist News Service gave the details of a study originally published in the Journal of Adolescent Health earlier that year. Serge Brand of the Psychiatric University Clinics in Basel, Switzerland, and his colleagues interviewed 113 teenagers (17-year old), 65 of whom reported having fallen in love recently.

The conclusion? The love-struck adolescents slept less, acted more compulsively more often, had "lots of ideas and creative energy", and were more likely to engage in risky behavior, such as reckless driving.

"'We were able to demonstrate that adolescents in early-stage intense romantic love did not differ from patients during a hypomanic stage,' say the researchers. This leads them to conclude that intense romantic love in teenagers is a 'psychopathologically prominent stage'".

But is it erotic lust or is it love that brings about these cerebral upheavals?

As distinct from love, lust is brought on by surges of sex hormones, such as testosterone and estrogen. These induce an indiscriminate scramble for physical gratification. In the brain, the hypothalamus (controls hunger, thirst, and other primordial drives) and the amygdala (the locus of arousal) become active. Attraction transpires once a more-or-less appropriate object is found (with the right body language and speed and tone of voice) and results in a panoply of sleep and eating disorders.

A recent study in the University of Chicago demonstrated that testosterone levels shoot up by one third even during a casual chat with a female stranger. The stronger the hormonal reaction, the more marked the changes in behavior, concluded the authors. This loop may be part of a larger "mating response". In animals, testosterone provokes aggression and recklessness. The hormone's readings in married men and fathers are markedly lower than in single males still "playing the field".

Still, the long-term outcomes of being in love are lustful. Dopamine, heavily secreted while falling in love, triggers the production of testosterone and sexual attraction then kicks in.

Helen Fisher of Rutger University suggests a three-phased model of falling in love. Each stage involves a distinct set of chemicals. The BBC summed it up succinctly and sensationally: "Events occurring in the brain when we are in love have similarities with mental illness".

Moreover, we are attracted to people with the same genetic makeup and smell (pheromones) of our parents. Dr Martha McClintock of the University of Chicago studied feminine attraction to sweaty T-shirts formerly worn by males. The closer the smell resembled her father's, the more attracted and aroused the woman became. Falling in love is, therefore, an exercise in proxy incest and a vindication of Freud's much-maligned Oedipus and Electra complexes.

Writing in the February 2004 issue of the journal NeuroImage, Andreas Bartels of University College London's Wellcome Department of Imaging Neuroscience described identical reactions in the brains of young mothers looking at their babies and in the brains of people looking at their lovers.

"Both romantic and maternal love are highly rewarding experiences that are linked to the perpetuation of the species, and consequently have a closely linked biological function of crucial evolutionary importance" - he told Reuters.

This incestuous backdrop of love was further demonstrated by psychologist David Perrett of the University of St Andrews in Scotland. The subjects in his experiments preferred their own faces - in other words, the composite of their two parents - when computer-morphed into the opposite sex.

Body secretions play a major role in the onslaught of love. In results published in February 2007 in the Journal of Neuroscience, researchers at the University of California at Berkeley demonstrated convincingly that women who sniffed androstadienone, a signaling chemical found in male sweat, saliva, and semen, experienced higher levels of the hormone cortisol. This results in sexual arousal and improved mood. The effect lasted a whopping one hour.

Still, contrary to prevailing misconceptions, love is mostly about negative emotions. As Professor Arthur Aron from State University of New York at Stonybrook has shown, in the first few meetings, people misinterpret certain physical cues and feelings - notably fear and thrill - as (falling in) love. Thus, counterintuitively, anxious people - especially those with the "serotonin transporter" gene - are more sexually active (i.e., fall in love more often).

Obsessive thoughts regarding the Loved One and compulsive acts are also common. Perception is distorted as is cognition. "Love is blind" and the lover easily fails the reality test. Falling in love involves the enhanced secretion of b-Phenylethylamine (PEA, or the "love chemical") in the first 2 to 4 years of the relationship.

This natural drug creates an euphoric high and helps obscure the failings and shortcomings of the potential mate. Such oblivion - perceiving only the spouse's good sides while discarding her bad ones - is a pathology akin to the primitive psychological defense mechanism known as "splitting". Narcissists - patients suffering from the [Narcissistic Personality Disorder](#) - also Idealize romantic or intimate partners. A similar cognitive-emotional impairment is common in many mental health conditions.

The activity of a host of neurotransmitters - such as Dopamine, Adrenaline (Norepinephrine), and Serotonin - is heightened (or in the case of Serotonin, lowered) in both paramours. Yet, such irregularities are also associated with Obsessive-Compulsive Disorder (OCD) and depression.

It is telling that once attachment is formed and infatuation gives way to a more stable and less exuberant relationship, the levels of these substances return to normal. They are replaced by two hormones (endorphins) which usually play a part in social interactions (including bonding and sex): Oxytocin (the "cuddling chemical") and Vasopressin. Oxytocin facilitates bonding. It is released in the mother during breastfeeding, in the members of the couple when they spend time together - and when they sexually climax. Viagra (sildenafil) seems to facilitate its release, at least in rats.

It seems, therefore, that the distinctions we often make between types of love - motherly love vs. romantic love, for instance - are artificial, as far as human biochemistry goes. As neuroscientist Larry Young's research with prairie voles at the Yerkes National Primate Research Center at Emory University demonstrates:

"(H)uman love is set off by a "biochemical chain of events" that originally evolved in ancient brain circuits involving mother-child bonding, which is stimulated in mammals by the release of oxytocin during labor, delivery and nursing."

He told the New-York Times ("Anti-Love Drug May Be Ticket to Bliss", January 12, 2009):

"Some of our sexuality has evolved to stimulate that same oxytocin system to create female-male bonds," Dr. Young said, noting that sexual foreplay and intercourse stimulate the same parts of a woman's body that are involved in giving birth and nursing. This hormonal hypothesis, which is by no means proven fact, would help explain a couple of differences between humans and less monogamous mammals: females' desire to have sex even when they are not fertile, and males' erotic fascination with breasts. More frequent sex and more attention to breasts, Dr. Young said, could help build long-term bonds through a " cocktail of ancient neuropeptides," like the oxytocin released during foreplay or orgasm. Researchers have achieved similar results by squirting oxytocin into people's nostrils..."

Moreover:

"A related hormone, vasopressin, creates urges for bonding and nesting when it is injected in male voles (or naturally activated by sex). After Dr. Young found that male voles with a genetically limited vasopressin response were less likely to find mates, Swedish researchers reported that men with a similar genetic tendency were less likely to get married ... 'If we give an oxytocin blocker to female voles, they become like 95 percent of other mammal species,' Dr. Young said. 'They will not bond no matter how many times they mate with a

male or hard how he tries to bond. *They mate, it feels really good and they move on if another male comes along. If love is similarly biochemically based, you should in theory be able to suppress it in a similar way.'"*

Love, in all its phases and manifestations, is an addiction, probably to the various forms of internally secreted norepinephrine, such as the aforementioned amphetamine-like PEA. Love, in other words, is a form of substance abuse. The withdrawal of romantic love has serious mental health repercussions.

A study conducted by Dr. Kenneth Kendler, professor of psychiatry and director of the Virginia Institute for Psychiatric and Behavioral Genetics, and others, and published in the September 2002 issue of *Archives of General Psychiatry*, revealed that breakups often lead to depression and anxiety. Other, fMRI-based studies, demonstrated how the insular cortex, in charge of experiencing pain, became active when subjects viewed photos of former loved ones.

Love and lust depend on context, as well as psychological makeup, or biochemistry: one can fall in and out love with the very same person (whose biochemistry, presumably, hasn't changed at all); the vast majority of one-night-standers reported that they did not find their partners sexually alluring: it was the opportunity that beckoned, not any specific attraction; similarly, the very same acts – kissing, hugging, even sexually explicit overtures – can be interpreted as innocuous, depending on who does what to whom and in which circumstances.

Indeed, love cannot be reduced to its biochemical and electrical components. Love is not tantamount to our bodily processes - rather, it is the way we *experience* them. Love is how we interpret these flows and ebbs of compounds using a higher-level language. In other words, love is pure poetry.

Interview granted to Readers' Digest - January 2009

"For what qualities in a man," asked the youth, "does a woman most ardently love him?" "For those qualities in him," replied the old tutor, "which his mother most ardently hates."

(A Book Without A Title, by George Jean Nathan (1918))

Q. The Top 5 Things Women Look for in a Man, the top five qualities (based on an American survey):

1. Good Judgment
2. Intelligence
3. Faithful
4. Affectionate
5. Financially Responsible

Why is this something women look for in men – why is it important?
How does this quality positively affect a relationship or marriage?
How do women recognize it?

A. There are three possible explanations as to why women look for these qualities in men: the evolutionary-biological one, the historical-cultural one, and the psychological-emotional one.

In evolutionary terms, good judgment and intelligence equal survival and the transmission of one's genes across the generations. Faithfulness and a sense of responsibility (financial and otherwise) guarantee that the woman's partner will persevere in the all-important tasks of homebuilding and childrearing. Finally, being affectionate cements the emotional bond between male and female and militates against potentially life-threatening maltreatment and abuse of the latter by the former.

From the historical-cultural point of view, most societies and cultures, well into the previous century, have been male-dominated and patriarchal. The male's judgment prevailed and his decisions dictated the course of the couple's life. An intelligent and financially responsible male provided a secure environment in which to raise children. The woman lived through her man, vicariously: his successes and failures reflected on her and determined her standing in society and her ability to develop and thrive on the personal level. His faithfulness and affections served to prevent competitors from usurping the female's place and thus threatening her male-dependent cosmos.

Granted, evolutionary constraints are anachronistic and social-cultural mores have changed: women, at least in Western societies, are now independent, both emotionally and economically. Yet, millennia of conditioned behavior cannot be eradicated in a few decades. Women continue to look in men for the qualities that used to matter in entirely different circumstances.

Finally, women are more level-headed when it comes to bonding. They tend to emphasize long-term relationships, based on reciprocity and the adhesive qualities of strong emotions. Good judgment, intelligence, and a developed sense of responsibility are crucial to the maintenance and preservation of functional, lasting, and durable couples - and so are faithfulness and being affectionate.

Soaring divorce rates and the rise of single parenthood prove that women are not good at recognizing the qualities they seek in men. It is not easy to tell apart the genuine article from the unctuous pretender. While intelligence (or lack thereof) can be discerned on a first date, it is difficult to predict traits such as faithfulness, good judgment, and reliability. Affections can really be mere affectations and women are sometimes so desperate for a mate that they delude themselves and treat their date as a [blank screen](#) onto which they project their wishes and needs.

Q. What are the top 5 Things Men Look for in a Woman, the top five qualities?

Why is this something men look for in women – why is it important?

How does this quality positively affect a relationship or marriage?

How do men recognize it?

A. From my experience and correspondence with thousands of couples, men seem to place a premium on these qualities in a woman:

1. Physical Attraction and Sexual Availability
2. Good-naturedness
3. Faithfulness
4. Protective Affectionateness
5. Dependability

There are three possible explanations as to why men look for these qualities in women: the evolutionary-biological one, the historical-cultural one, and the psychological-emotional one.

In evolutionary terms, physical attractiveness denotes good underlying health and genetic-immunological compatibility. These guarantee the efficacious transmission of one's genes to future generations. Of course, having sex is a precondition for bearing children and, so, sexual availability is important, but only when it is coupled with faithfulness: men are loth to raise and invest scarce resource in someone else's progeny. Dependable women are more likely to propagate the species, so they are desirable. Finally, men and women are likely to do a better job of raising a family if the woman is good-natured, easy-going, adaptable, affectionate, and mothering. These qualities cement the emotional bond between male and female and prevent potentially life-threatening maltreatment and abuse of the latter by the former.

From the historical-cultural point of view, most societies and cultures, well into the previous century, have been male-dominated and patriarchal. Women were treated as chattels or possessions, an extension of the male. The "ownership" of an attractive female advertised to the world the male's prowess and desirability. Her good nature, affectionateness, and protectiveness proved that her man was a worthwhile "catch" and elevated his social status. Her dependability and faithfulness allowed him to embark on long trips or complex, long-term undertakings without the distractions of emotional uncertainty and the anxieties of letdown and betrayal.

Finally, men are more cavalier when it comes to bonding. They tend to maintain both long-term and short-term relationships and are, therefore, far less exclusive and monogamous than women. They are more concerned with what they are getting out of a relationship than with reciprocity and, though they often feel as strongly as women and can be equally romantic, their emotional landscape and expression are more constrained and they sometimes confuse love with possessiveness or even codependence. Thus, men tend to emphasize the external (physical attraction) and the functional (good-naturedness, faithfulness, reliability) over the internal and the purely emotional.

Soaring divorce rates and the rise of single parenthood prove that men are not good at recognizing the qualities they seek in women. It is not easy to tell apart the genuine article from the unctuous pretender. While physical attractiveness (or lack thereof) can be discerned on a first date, it is difficult to predict traits such as faithfulness, good-naturedness, and reliability. Affections can really be mere affectations and men are sometimes such narcissistic navel-gazers that they delude themselves and treat their date as a blank screen onto which they project their wishes and needs.

On the Incest Taboo: Incest as an Autoerotic Social and Cultural Act

"...An experience with an adult may seem merely a curious and pointless game, or it may be a hideous trauma leaving lifelong psychic scars. In many cases the reaction of parents and society determines the child's interpretation of the event. What would have been a trivial and soon-forgotten act becomes traumatic if the mother cries, the father rages, and the police interrogate the child."

(Encyclopedia Britannica, 2004 Edition)

In contemporary thought, incest is invariably associated with child abuse and its horrific, long-lasting, and often irreversible consequences. Incest is not such a clear-cut matter as it has been made out to be over millennia of taboo. Many participants claim to have enjoyed the act and its physical and emotional consequences. It is often the result of seduction. In some cases, two consenting and fully informed adults are involved.

Many types of relationships, which are defined as incestuous, are between genetically unrelated parties (a stepfather and a daughter), or between fictive kin or between classificatory kin (that belong to the same matriline or patriline). In certain societies (the Native American or the Chinese) it is sufficient to carry the same family name (=to belong to the same clan) and marriage is forbidden.

Some incest prohibitions relate to sexual acts - others to marriage. In some societies, incest is mandatory or prohibited, according to the social class or particular circumstances (Ugarit, Bali, Papua New Guinea, Polynesian and Melanesian islands). In others, the Royal House started a tradition of incestuous marriages, which was later imitated by lower classes (Ancient Egypt, Hawaii, Pre-Columbian Mixtec). Some societies are more tolerant of consensual incest than others (Japan, India until the 1930's, Australia).

The list is long and it serves to demonstrate the diversity of attitudes towards this most universal of taboos. Generally put, we can say that a prohibition to have sex with or marry a related person should be classified as an incest prohibition.

Perhaps the strongest feature of incest has been hitherto downplayed: that it is, essentially, an ***autoerotic act***.

Having sex with a first-degree blood relative is like having sex with oneself. It is a Narcissistic act and like all acts Narcissistic, it involves the objectification of the partner. The incestuous Narcissist over-values and then devalues his sexual partner. He is devoid of empathy (cannot see the other's point of view or put himself in her shoes).

For an in depth treatment of <u>narcissism</u> and its psychosexual dimension, see these (click on the links):

<u>*Narcissistic and Psychopathic Parents and Their Children*</u>

<u>*Narcissistic Personality Disorder (NPD) and Pathological Narcissism FAQs*</u>

<u>*Personality disorders FAQs*</u>

Paradoxically, it is the reaction of society that transforms incest into such a disruptive phenomenon. The condemnation, the horror, the revulsion and the attendant social sanctions interfere with the internal processes and dynamics of the incestuous family. It is from society that the child learns that something is horribly wrong, that he should feel guilty, and that the offending parent is a defective role model.

As a direct result, the formation of the child's Superego is stunted and it remains infantile, ideal, sadistic, perfectionist, demanding and punishing. The child's Ego, on the other hand, is likely to be replaced by a False Ego version, whose job it is to suffer the social consequences of the hideous act.

To sum up: society's reactions in the case of incest are pathogenic and are most likely to produce a Narcissistic or a Borderline patient. Dysempathic, exploitative, emotionally labile, immature, and in eternal search for Narcissistic Supply – the child becomes a replica of his incestuous and socially-castigated parent.

If so, why did human societies develop such pathogenic responses? In other words, why is incest considered a taboo in all known human collectives and cultures? Why are incestuous liaisons treated so harshly and punitively?

Freud said that incest provokes horror because it touches upon our forbidden, ambivalent emotions towards members of our close family. This ambivalence covers both aggression towards other members (forbidden and punishable) and (sexual) attraction to them (doubly forbidden and punishable).

Edward Westermarck proffered an opposite view that the domestic proximity of the members of the family breeds sexual repulsion (the epigenetic rule known as the Westermarck effect) to counter naturally occurring genetic sexual attraction. The incest taboo simply reflects emotional and biological realities within the family rather than aiming to restrain the inbred instincts of its members, claimed Westermarck.

Though much-disputed by geneticists, some scholars maintain that the incest taboo may have been originally designed to prevent the degeneration of the genetic stock of the clan or tribe through intra-family breeding (closed endogamy). But, even if true, this no longer applies. In today's world incest rarely results in pregnancy and the transmission of genetic material. Sex today is about recreation as much as procreation.

Good contraceptives should, therefore, encourage incestuous, couples. In many other species inbreeding or straightforward incest are the norm. Finally, in most countries, incest prohibitions apply also to non-genetically-related people.

It seems, therefore, that the incest taboo was and is aimed at one thing in particular: to preserve the family unit and its proper functioning.

Incest is more than a mere manifestation of a given personality disorder or a paraphilia (incest is considered by many to be a subtype of pedophilia). It harks back to the very nature of the family. It is closely entangled with its functions and with its contribution to the development of the individual within it.

The family is an efficient venue for the transmission of accumulated property as well as information - both horizontally (among family members) and vertically (down the generations). The process of socialization largely relies on these familial mechanisms, making the family the most important agent of socialization by far.

The family is a mechanism for the allocation of genetic and material wealth. Worldly goods are passed on from one generation to the next through succession, inheritance and residence. Genetic material is handed down through the sexual act. It is the mandate of the family to increase both by accumulating property and by marrying outside the family (exogamy).

Clearly, incest prevents both. It preserves a limited genetic pool and makes an increase of material possessions through intermarriage all but impossible.

The family's roles are not merely materialistic, though.

One of the main businesses of the family is to teach to its members self control, self regulation and healthy adaptation. Family members share space and resources and siblings share the mother's emotions and attention. Similarly, the family educates its young members to master their drives and to postpone the self-gratification which attaches to acting upon them.

The incest taboo conditions children to control their erotic drive by abstaining from ingratiating themselves with members of the opposite sex within the same family. There could be little question that incest constitutes a lack of control and impedes the proper separation of impulse (or stimulus) from action.

Additionally, incest probably interferes with the defensive aspects of the family's existence. It is through the family that aggression is legitimately channeled, expressed and externalized. By imposing discipline and hierarchy on its members, the family is transformed into a cohesive and efficient war machine. It absorbs economic resources, social status and members of other families. It forms alliances and fights other clans over scarce goods, tangible and intangible.

This efficacy is undermined by incest. It is virtually impossible to maintain discipline and hierarchy in an incestuous family where some members assume sexual roles not normally theirs. Sex is an expression of power – emotional and physical. The members of the family involved in incest surrender power and assume it out of the regular flow patterns that have made the family the formidable apparatus that it is.

These new power politics weaken the family, both internally and externally. Internally, emotive reactions (such as the jealousy of other family members) and clashing authorities and responsibilities are likely to undo the delicate unit. Externally, the family is vulnerable to ostracism and more official forms of intervention and dismantling.

Finally, the family is an identity endowment mechanism. It bestows identity upon its members. Internally, the members of the family derive meaning from their position in the family tree and its "organization chart" (which conform to societal expectations and norms). Externally, through exogamy, by incorporating "strangers", the family absorbs other identities and thus enhances social solidarity (Claude Levy-Strauss) at the expense of the solidarity of the nuclear, original family.

Exogamy, as often noted, allows for the creation of extended alliances. The "identity creep" of the family is in total opposition to incest. The latter increases the solidarity and cohesiveness of the incestuous family – but at the expense of its ability to digest and absorb other identities of other family units. Incest, in other words, adversely affects social cohesion and solidarity.

Lastly, as aforementioned, incest interferes with well-established and rigid patterns of inheritance and property allocation. Such disruption is likely to have led in primitive societies to disputes and conflicts - including armed clashes and deaths. To prevent such recurrent and costly bloodshed was one of the intentions of the incest taboo.

The more primitive the society, the more strict and elaborate the set of incest prohibitions and the fiercer the reactions of society to violations. It appears that the less violent the dispute settlement methods and mechanisms in a given culture – the more lenient the attitude to incest.

The incest taboo is, therefore, a cultural trait. Protective of the efficient mechanism of the family, society sought to minimize disruption to its activities and to the clear flows of authority, responsibilities, material wealth and information horizontally and vertically.

Incest threatened to unravel this magnificent creation - the family. Alarmed by the possible consequences (internal and external feuds, a rise in the level of aggression and violence) – society introduced the taboo. It came replete with physical and emotional sanctions: stigmatization, revulsion and horror, imprisonment, the demolition of the errant and socially mutant family cell.

As long as societies revolve around the relegation of power, its sharing, its acquisition and dispensation – there will always exist an incest taboo. But in a different societal and cultural setting, it is conceivable not to have such a taboo. We can easily imagine a society where incest is extolled, taught, and practiced - and out-breeding is regarded with horror and revulsion.

The incestuous marriages among members of the royal households of Europe were intended to preserve the familial property and expand the clan's territory. They were normative, not aberrant. Marrying an outsider was considered abhorrent.

An incestuous society - where incest is the norm - is conceivable even today.

Two out of many possible scenarios:

1. *"The Lot Scenario"*

A plague or some other natural disaster decimate the population of planet Earth. People remain alive only in isolated clusters, co-habiting only with their closest kin. Surely incestuous procreation is preferable to virtuous extermination. Incest becomes normative.

Incest is as entrenched a taboo as cannibalism. Yet, it is better to eat the flesh of your dead football team mates than perish high up on the Andes (a harrowing tale of survival recounted in the book and eponymous film, "Alive").

2. The Egyptian Scenario

Resources become so scarce that family units scramble to keep them exclusively within the clan.

Exogamy - marrying outside the clan - amounts to a unilateral transfer of scarce resources to outsiders and strangers. Incest becomes an economic imperative.

An incestuous society would be either utopian or dystopian, depending on the reader's point of view - but that it is possible is doubtless.

Pedophilia and Fetishism: Sexual Paraphilias

1. Pedophilia

Click HERE to [Watch]() the Video

Pedophiles are attracted to prepubescent children and act on their sexual fantasies. It is a startling fact that the etiology of this paraphilia is unknown. Pedophiles come from all walks of life and have no common socio-economic background. Contrary to media-propagated myths, most of them had not been sexually abused in childhood and the vast majority of pedophiles are also drawn to adults of the opposite sex (are heterosexuals).

Only a few belong to the Exclusive Type - the ones who are tempted solely by kids. Nine tenths of all pedophiles are male. They are fascinated by preteen females, teenage males, or (more rarely) both.

Moreover, at least one fifth (and probably more) of the population have pedophiliac fantasies. The prevalence of child pornography and child prostitution prove it. Pedophiles start out as "normal" people and are profoundly shocked and distressed to discover their illicit sexual preference for the prepubertal. The process and mechanisms of transition from socially acceptable sexuality to much-condemned (and criminal) pedophilia are still largely mysterious.

Pedophiles seem to have [narcissistic]() and [antisocial (psychopathic)]() traits. They lack [empathy]() for their victims and express no remorse for their actions. They are in [denial]() and, being [pathological confabulators](), they rationalize their transgressions, claiming that the children were merely being educated for their own good and, anyhow, derived great pleasure from it.

The pedophile's ego-syntony rests on his [alloplastic defenses](). He generally tends to blame others (or the world or the "system") for his misfortunes, failures, and deficiencies.Pedophiles frequently accuse their victims of acting promiscuously, of "coming on to them", of actively tempting, provoking, and luring (or even trapping) them.

The pedophile - similar to the [autistic patient]() - misinterprets the child's body language and inter-personal cues. His social communication skills are impaired and he fails to adjust information gained to the surrounding circumstances (for instance, to the kid's age and maturity).

Coupled with his lack of empathy, this recurrent inability to truly comprehend others cause the pedophile to objectify the targets of his lasciviousness. Pedophilia is, in essence, auto-erotic. The pedophile uses children's bodies to masturbate with. Hence the success of the Internet among pedophiles: it offers disembodied, anonymous, masturbatory sex. Children in cyberspace are mere representations - often nothing more than erotic photos and screen names.

It is crucial to realize that pedophiles are not enticed by the children themselves, by their bodies, or by their budding and nubile sexuality (remember Nabokov's Lolita?). Rather, pedophiles are drawn to what children symbolize, to what preadolescents stand for and represent. With the advent of Feminism and gender-equality, women have lost their traditional role as socially-acceptable and permissible sexual "child-substitutes" (except in Japan). This social upheaval may account for the rise in pedophilia across the world.

To the pedophile ...

I. Sex with children is "free" and "daring"

Sex with subteens implies freedom of action with impunity. It enhances the pedophile's magical sense of omnipotence and immunity. By defying the authority of the state and the edicts of his culture and society, the pedophile experiences an adrenaline rush to which he gradually becomes addicted. Illicit sex becomes the outlet for his urgent need to live dangerously and recklessly.

The pedophile is on a quest to reassert control over his life. Studies have consistently shown that pedophilia is associated with anomic states (war, famine, epidemics) and with major life crises (failure, relocation, infidelity of spouse, separation, divorce, unemployment, bankruptcy, illness, death of the offender's nearest and dearest).

It is likely - though hitherto unsubstantiated by research - that the typical pedophile is depressive and with a borderline personality (low organization and fuzzy personal boundaries). Pedophiles are reckless and emotionally labile. The pedophile's sense of self-worth is volatile and dysregulated. He is likely to suffer from abandonment anxiety and be a codependent or counterdependent.

Paradoxically, it is by seemingly losing control in one aspect of his life (sex) that the pedophile re-acquires a sense of mastery. The same mechanism is at work in the development of eating disorders. An inhibitory deficit is somehow magically perceived as omnipotence.

II. Sex with children is corrupt and decadent

The pedophile makes frequent (though unconscious) use of projection and projective identification in his relationships with children. He makes his victims treat him the way he views himself - or attributes to them traits and behaviors that are truly his.

The pedophile is aware of society's view of his actions as vile, corrupt, forbidden, evil, and decadent (especially if the pedophiliac act involves incest). He derives pleasure from the sleazy nature of his pursuits because it tends to sustain his view of himself as "bad", "a failure", "deserving of punishment", and "guilty".

In extreme (mercifully uncommon) cases, the pedophile projects these torturous feelings and self-perceptions onto his victims. The children defiled and abused by his sexual attentions thus become "rotten", "bad objects", guilty and punishable. This leads to sexual sadism, lust rape, and snuff murders.

III. Sex with children is a reenactment of a painful past

Many pedophiles truly bond with their prey. To them, children are the reification of innocence, genuineness, trust, and faithfulness - qualities that the pedophile wishes to nostalgically recapture.

The relationship with the child provides the pedophile with a "safe passage" to his own, repressed and fearful, inner child. Through his victim, the pedophile gains access to his suppressed and thwarted emotions. It is a fantasy-like second chance to reenact his childhood, this time benignly. The pedophile's dream to make peace with his past comes true transforming the interaction with the child to an exercise in wish fulfillment.

IV. Sex with children is a shared psychosis

The pedophile treats "his" chosen child as an object, an extension of himself, devoid of a separate existence and denuded of distinct needs. He finds the child's submissiveness and gullibility gratifying. He frowns on any sign of personal autonomy and regards it as a threat. By intimidating, cajoling, charming, and making false promises, the abuser isolates his prey from his family, school, peers, and from the rest of society and, thus, makes the child's dependence on him total.

To the pedophile, the child is a "transitional object" - a training ground on which to exercise his adult relationship skills. The pedophile erroneously feels that the child will never betray and abandon him, therefore guaranteeing "object constancy".

The pedophile – stealthily but unfailingly – exploits the vulnerabilities in the psychological makeup of his victim. The child may have low self-esteem, a fluctuating sense of self-worth, primitive defence mechanisms, phobias, mental health problems, a disability, a history of failure, bad relations with parents, siblings, teachers, or peers, or a tendency to blame herself, or to feel inadequate (autoplastic neurosis). The kid may come from an abusive family or environment – which conditioned her or him to expect abuse as inevitable and "normal". In extreme and rare cases – the victim is a masochist, possessed of an urge to seek ill-treatment and pain.

The pedophile is the guru at the center of a cult. Like other gurus, he demands complete obedience from his "partner". He feels entitled to adulation and special treatment by his child-mate. He punishes the wayward and the straying lambs. He enforces discipline.

The child finds himself in a twilight zone. The pedophile imposes on him a shared psychosis, replete with persecutory delusions, "enemies", mythical narratives, and apocalyptic scenarios if he is flouted. The child is rendered the joint guardian of a horrible secret.

The pedophile's control is based on ambiguity, unpredictability, fuzziness, and ambient abuse. His ever-shifting whims exclusively define right versus wrong, desirable and unwanted, what is to be pursued and what to be avoided. He alone determines rights and obligations and alters them at will.

The typical pedophile is a micro-manager. He exerts control over the minutest details and behaviors. He punishes severely and abuses withholders of information and those who fail to conform to his wishes and goals.

The pedophile does not respect the boundaries and privacy of the (often reluctant and terrified) child. He ignores his or her wishes and treats children as objects or instruments of gratification. He seeks to control both situations and people compulsively.

The pedophile acts in a patronizing and condescending manner and criticizes often. He alternates between emphasizing the minutest faults (devalues) and exaggerating the looks, talents, traits, and skills (idealizes) of the child. He is wildly unrealistic in his expectations – which legitimizes his subsequent abusive conduct.

Narcissistic pedophiles claim to be infallible, superior, talented, skillful, omnipotent, and omniscient. They often lie and confabulate to support these unfounded claims and to justify their actions. Most pedophiles suffer from cognitive deficits and reinterpret reality to fit their fantasies.

In extreme cases, the pedophile feels above the law – any kind of law. This grandiose and haughty conviction leads to criminal acts, incestuous or polygamous relationships, and recurrent friction with the authorities.

V. The pedophile regards sex with children as an ego-booster

Subteen children are, by definition, "inferior". They are physically weaker, dependent on others for the fulfillment of many of their needs, cognitively and emotionally immature, and easily manipulated. Their fund of knowledge is limited and their skills restricted. His relationships with children buttress the pedophile's twin grandiose delusions of omnipotence and omniscience. Compared to his victims, the pedophiles is always the stronger, the wiser, the most skillful and well-informed.

VI. Sex with children guarantees companionship

Inevitably, the pedophile considers his child-victims to be his best friends and companions. Pedophiles are lonely, erotomanic, people.

The pedophile believes that he is in love with (or simply loves) the child. Sex is merely one way to communicate his affection and caring. But there are other venues.

To show his keen interest, the common pedophile keeps calling the child, dropping by, writing e-mails, giving gifts, providing services, doing unsolicited errands "on the kid's behalf", getting into relationships with the preteen's parents, friends, teachers, and peers, and, in general, making himself available (stalking) at all times. The pedophile feels free to make legal, financial, and emotional decisions for the child.

The pedophile intrudes on the victim's privacy, disrespects the child's express wishes and personal boundaries and ignores his or her emotions, needs, and preferences. To thepedophile, "love" means enmeshment and clinging coupled with an overpowering separation anxiety (fear of being abandoned).

Moreover, no amount of denials, chastising, threats, and even outright hostile actions convince the erotomaniac that the child not in love with him. He knows better and will make the world see the light as well. The child and his guardians are simply unaware of what is good for the kid. The pedophile determinedly sees it as his or her task to bring life and happiness into the child's dreary and unhappy existence.

Thus, regardless of overwhelming evidence to the contrary, the pedophile is convinced that his feelings are reciprocated - in other words, that the child is equally infatuated with him or her. He interprets everything the child does (or refrains from doing) as coded messages confessing to and conveying the child's interest in and eternal devotion to thepedophile and to the "relationship".

Some (by no means all) pedophiles are socially-inapt, awkward, schizoid, and suffer from a host of mood and anxiety disorders. They may also be legitimately involved with the child (e.g., stepfather, former spouse, teacher, gym instructor, sibling) - or with his parents (for instance, a former boyfriend, a one night stand, colleagues or co-workers). They are driven by their all-consuming loneliness and all-pervasive fantasies.

Consequently, pedophiles react badly to any perceived rejection by their victims. They turn on a dime and become dangerously vindictive, out to destroy the source of their mounting frustration. When the "relationship" looks hopeless, some pedophiles violently embark on a spree of self-destruction.

Pedophilia is to some extent a culture-bound syndrome, defined as it is by the chronological age of the child involved. Ephebophilia, for instance - the exclusive sexual infatuation with teenagers - is not considered to be a form of pedophilia (or even paraphilia). The very idea of impermissible (and, later, illegal) sex with children has emerged in the West hand in hand with the novel concept of childhood. As Western dominance and values spread globally, so did Western mores and ethics.

In some cultures, societies and countries (Afghanistan, for instance) the age of consent is as low as 12. The marriageable age in Britain until the end of the nineteenth century was 10. Sex and genital foreplay with children was common, encouraged and even medically-prescribed literally all over the world until 150 years ago. Incest and pedophilia were often linked and sanctioned.

Various religious texts – including the Jewish Talmud, surprisingly progressive for its time – permit sexual relations, including incest, as early as age 3 (for a girl) or 8 (for a boy).Pedophilia was and is a common and socially-condoned practice in certain tribal societies and isolated communities (the Island of Pitcairn).

It would, therefore, be wise to redefine pedophilia as an attraction to or sexual acts with prepubescent children or with people of the equivalent mental age (e.g., retarded) in contravention of social, legal, and cultural accepted practices.

The committee that is writing the next edition of the Diagnostic and Statistical Manual (DSM) is considering to render hebephilia (when adults are sexually attracted to teenagers around the time of puberty) a subtype of pedophilia and to rename it pedohebephilia.

"The rows over hebephilia and paraphilic coercive disorder aren't academic, because 20 US states have passed laws that allow sex offenders who have served their sentences to be detained indefinitely in a secure hospital if they are deemed "sexual predators" (New Scientist, 24 February 2007, p 6). This can only be done if the offenders have a psychiatric disorder that increases their risk of reoffending - which few do, according to DSM-IV. (A critic) says that if hebephilia and paraphilic coercive disorder make it into DSM-V, they will be seized upon to consign men to a lifetime of incarceration." (New Scientist, "Psychiatry's Civil War", December 2009)

2. Sexual Fetishism: The Object is Desire

The sexual fetish is like "the fetich in which the savage sees the embodiment of his god"

S. Freud, "Three Contributions to the Theory of Sex" (1905)

A. The Disorder

The propensity to regard and treat other people (caregivers, parents) as objects (to "objectify" them) is an inevitable phase of personal development and growth during the formative years (6 months to 3 years). As psychoanalysis and the Object Relations school of psychology teach us, we outgrow this immature way of relating to our human environment and instead develop a sense of empathy.

Yet, some of us remain "fixated" and do not progress into full-fledged adulthood. Arguably the most ostentatious manifestation of such retardation is the sexual paraphilia known as fetishism.

There are three types of fetishes:

I. An inanimate object, usually with a sexual connotation (such as a bra);

II. A **body part** that is clearly still connected to a complete body, dead or alive (e.g., hair, feet);

III. A **reified trait**, usually a deformity or idiosyncrasy that implies inferiority, helplessness, or dependence (for instance, a lame, or grotesquely obese, or hunchbacked person).

Consequently, there are three categories of fetishism and fetishists:

I. **Objective fetishists**, for whom the inanimate fetish stands for and symbolizes a desired whole that is out of reach;

II. **Somatic fetishists**, for whom the body part stands for and symbolizes a coveted human body (and, by extension, a relationship) that is unattainable;

III. **Abstract fetishists**, who latch on to a trait or a characteristic as a means to indirectly interact with their "defective" bearer and thus fulfill the fetishist's grandiose fantasies of omnipotence and innate superiority (pathological narcissism).

Arguably, people who prefer autoerotic, partialist, necrophilic, coprophilic, urophilic, or anonymous sex are also fetishists with the fetish being their own bodies or the organs or excretions of their sex partners.

Sexual fetishism is predicated on a pathological sexual attachment to a fetish. The fetishist climaxes only in the presence of the fetish and cannot reach orgasm otherwise. In the absence of their fetish, most fetishists are sexually dysfunctional (for instance, they suffer from erectile dysfunction or are sexually hypoactive). Some forms of fetishism involves sado-masochistic and domination/submission fantasies (with fetishes such as feet or boots and shoes).

The circumstances surrounding the sexual encounter are immaterial to the fetishist, as is his environment. Thus, a fetishist who is fixated on bras or feet is unlikely to mind the physical characteristics of the proprietress of either.

This "tunnel vision" is common to other mental health disorders, such as the autistic spectrum, schizophrenic, or somatoform ones. It may indicate the existence of underlying mental health problems or traumas that either give rise or exacerbate fetishism.

Fetishism can be confined to recurrent and intense fantasies and urges, or acted upon (behavioral). It invariably involves masturbation. The fetishist interacts with his fetish in five ways: by watching it (worn by a sex partner or as an isolated item); by holding it; by rubbing it or against it; by smelling it; and by vividly fantasizing about it.

B. Etiology

The fetish has to be "exactly right" in smell, texture, and appearance. Fetishists often go to great length to make sure that their fetish is just "the way it should be". It would seem that fetishes are "triggers", akin to objects that provoke flashbacks and panic attacks in the post-traumatic stress disorder. It stands to reason, therefore, that the same mental mechanism gives rise to both: association of learning.

Memory has been proven to be state-dependent: information learnt in specific mental, physical, or emotional states is most easily recalled in similar states. Conversely, in a process known as redintegration, mental and emotional states are completely invoked and restored when only a single element is encountered and experienced (a smell, a taste, a sight).

In 1877, the French psychologist Alfred Binet (1857-1911) suggested that fetishism is the outcome of a repeated co-occurrence of an object (the fetish) and sexual arousal. The more frequent the association, the more entrenched, persistent, and enhanced it becomes (i.e., the stronger the allure of the fetish and the more secure its exclusivity as a modus of sexual expression).

Behaviorist psychologists largely concurred with Binet, though they preferred to use the term "conditioning", rather than "association". Others (Wilson, 1981) suggested that fetishism is nothing but faulty imprinting. Yet, imprinting has never been demonstrated in humans and fetishists, whatever we may think of their predilections, are human beings.

Fetishes gain in strength when other avenues of sexual gratification are not available owing to extreme shyness, fear of sex, a physiological dysfunction, or socio-cultural inhibitions. Thus, fetishism should be more prevalent in sexually repressive cultures and societies and among women, homosexuals, and other sexual minorities. Yet, fetishism has been noted mostly among men, both homosexual and heterosexual. The phenomenon may go under-reported among women, though.

Western society encourages what the sexologist Magnus Hirschfeld called "partial attractiveness". Women are taught to emphasize certain organs and areas of their body, particular fashion accessories and clothing items, and gender-specific traits. These serve as "healthy and socially-acceptable fetishes" to which males respond.

Other "explanations" of fetishism are so convoluted that they either defy reason or cannot be regarded as science by any stretch of the word. Thus, Freud suggested (Standard Edition, Vol. 21, pp. 147-157, 1927) that fetishism is the outcome of an unresolved castration anxiety in childhood. The fetishist attempts to ward off the lingering stress by maintaining unconsciously that women are really possessed of an occult penis and are, thus, made "whole". Fetishes, in other words, are symbolic representations of phalli.

In his article "Splitting of the Ego in the Process of Defense" (Standard Edition, Vol. 23, pp. 275-8), Freud offered yet another mechanism. He postulated that the fetishist's Egoharbors two coexistent, fully functional, and hermetically sealed "attitudes" towards external reality: one taking the world into account and the other ignoring it.

Adherents of the Object Relations school of psychodynamics, such as Donald Winnicott, consider fetishes to be "transitional objects" that outgrew their usefulness. The fetish originally allowed the child to derive comfort and compensate for the withdrawal of the Primary Object (the mother, or caregiver). Winnicott, too, believes that the fetish amounts to an anxiety-ameliorating substitute for the missing maternal phallus.

Psychosexual Stages of Personal Development

The Viennese neurologist, Sigmund Freud, was among the first to offer a model of psychological development in early childhood (within the framework of psychoanalysis). He closely linked the sex drive (libido) to the formation of personality and described five psychosexual stages, four of which are centered around various erogenous zones in the body.

The pursuit of pleasure ("the pleasure principle") and the avoidance of pain drive the infant to explore his or her self and the world at large. Pleasure is inextricably linked to sexual gratification. In the oral phase (from birth to 24 months), the baby focuses on the tongue, lips, and mouth and derives gratification from breast feeding, thumb sucking, biting, swallowing, and other oral exploratory activities.

This is naturally followed by the anal stage (24 to 36 months). The baby immensely enjoys defecation and related bowel movements. But it is also the first time in his or her life that the toddler is subjected to the censure and displeasure of caretakers. Hitherto unconditionally adoring adults now demand that the infant delay gratification, relieve himself only in the bathroom, and not play with his feces. This experience - of hitherto unprecedented adult approbation - can be traumatic.

The phallic stage (age 3 to 6 years) involves the discovery of the penis and clitoris as foci of pleasurable experience. This tantalizing novelty is coupled with sexual desire directed at the parent of the opposite sex (boys are attracted to their mothers and girls, to their fathers). The child overtly and covertly competes with the same-sex parent for the desired parent's attention: boys joust with their fathers and girls with their mothers. These are the famous Oedipal and Electra complexes.

If the parent is insufficiently mature or narcissistic and encourages the attentions of the child in acts of covert (emotional) and overt (physical) incest, it could lead to the development of certain mental health disorders, among them the Histrionic, Narcissistic, and Borderline personality disorders. Doting, over-indulgence, and smothering are, therefore, forms of child abuse. Sexual innuendo, treating the child as an adult or substitute partner, or regarding one's offspring as an extension of one's self also constitute abusive conduct.

The phallic stage is followed by 6 to 7 years of latent sexuality that is rekindled in puberty. Adolescence is a period of personal development labeled by Freud the genital phase. In the previous rungs of psychosexual evolution, the child's own body was the source of sexual pleasure. Hitherto, the adolescent and young adult seeks sexual gratification from and invests sexual energy in others. This object-relatedness is what we call mature love.

Sex and Personality Disorders

Our sexual behavior expresses not only our psychosexual makeup but also the entirety of our personality. Sex is the one realm of conduct which involves the full gamut of emotions, cognitions, socialization, traits, heredity, and learned and acquired behaviors. By observing one's sexual predilections and acts, the trained psychotherapist and diagnostician can learn a lot about the patient.

Inevitably, the sexuality of patients with personality disorders is thwarted and stunted. In the Paranoid Personality Disorder, sex is depersonalized and the sexual partner is dehumanized. The paranoid is besieged by persecutory delusions and equates intimacy with life-threatening vulnerability, a "breach in the defenses" as it were. the paranoid uses sex to reassure himself that he is still in control and to quell is anxiety.

The patient with Schizoid Personality Disorder is asexual. The schizoid is not interested in maintaining any kind of relationship and avoids interactions with others - including sexual encounters. He prefers solitude and solitary activities to any excitement sex can offer. The Schizotypal Personality Disorder and the Avoidant Personality Disorder have a similar effect on the patient but for different reasons: the schizotypal is acutely discomfited by intimacy and avoids close relationships in which his oddness and eccentricity will be revealed and, inevitably, derided or decried. The Avoidant remains aloof and a recluse in order to conceal her self-perceived shortcomings and flaws. The avoidant mortally fears rejection and criticism. The schizoid's asexuality is a result of indifference - the schizotypal's and avoidant's, the outcome of social anxiety.

Patients with the Histrionic Personality Disorder (mostly women) leverage their body, appearance, sex appeal, and sexuality to gain narcissistic supply (attention) and to secure attachment, however fleeting. Sex is used by histrionics to prop up their self-esteem and to regulate their labile sense of self-worth. Histrionics are, therefore, "inappropriately seductive" and have multiple sexual liaisons and partners.

The sexual behavior of histrionics is virtually indistinguishable from that of the somatic narcissist (patient with Narcissistic Personality Disorder) and the psychopath (patient with Antisocial Personality Disorder). But while the histrionic is overly-emotional, invested in intimacy, and self-dramatizing ("drama queen"), the somatic narcissist and the psychopath are cold and calculating.

The Somatic narcissist and the psychopath use their partners' bodies to masturbate with and their sexual conquests serve merely to prop up their wavering self-confidence (somatic narcissist) or to satisfy a physiological need (psychopath). The somatic narcissist and psychopath have no sexual playmates - only sexual playthings. Having conquered the target, they discard it, withdraw and move on heartlessly.

The cerebral narcissist is indistinguishable from the schizoid: he is asexual and prefers activities and interactions which emphasize his intelligence or intellectual achievements. Many cerebral narcissists are celibate even when married.

Patients with the Borderline Personality Disorder and the Dependent Personality Disorder both suffer from abandonment and separation anxieties and are clinging, demanding, and emotionally labile - but their sexual behavior is distinguishable. The borderline uses her sexuality to reward or punish her mate. The dependent uses it to "enslave" and condition her lover or spouse. The borderline withholds sex or offers it in accordance with the ups and downs of her tumultuous and vicissitudinal relationships. The codependent tries to make her mate addicted to her particular brand of sexuality: submissive, faintly masochistic, and experimental.

Narcissists, Sex and Fidelity: The Somatic and the Cerebral Narcissist

Cerebral narcissists use their intellect, intelligence, and verbal skills to derive narcissistic supply. Somatic narcissists leverage their body and sexuality to secure an uninterrupted flow of supply.

Each narcissist is either predominantly cerebral or somatic, but there is no type-constancy: the dominant type gives way to the recessive type in times of scarce, deficient, or absent supply (for instance: following a major life crisis).

Question:

Are narcissists mostly hyperactive or hypoactive sexually and to what extent are they likely to be unfaithful in marriage?

Answer:

Broadly speaking, there are two types of narcissists, loosely corresponding to the two categories mentioned in the question: the somatic narcissist and the cerebral narcissist.

The somatic narcissist derives narcissistic supply from other people's reactions to his body: sexual conquests, bodybuilding, athletic prowess, competence in outdoor activities, or mere preening and titivating. Cerebral narcissists flaunt their intellect, intelligence, and knowledge to secure attention and adulation.

Whether one becomes a somatic narcissist or a cerebral one depends on one's upbringing as a child. If the infant is taught that it can secure the parents' love only by being intellectually brilliant - it becomes a cerebral narcissist. If it is conditioned to excel in sports or outdoor activities and to compete for sexual conquests as a prerequisite for being loved, it becomes somatic.

Narcissists are misogynists. They hold women in contempt, they loathe and fear them. They seek to torment and frustrate them (either by debasing them sexually - or by withholding sex from them). They harbor ambiguous feelings towards the sexual act.

The somatic narcissist uses sex to "conquer" and "secure" new sources of narcissistic supply. Consequently, the somatic rarely gets emotionally-involved with his "targets". His is a mechanical act, devoid of intimacy and commitment. The cerebral narcissist feels that sex is demeaning and degrading. Acting on one's sex drive is a primitive, basic, and common impulse. The cerebral narcissist convinces himself that he is above all that, endowed as he is with superior intelligence and superhuman self-control.

Still, sex for both types of narcissists is an instrument designed to increase the number of Sources of Narcissistic Supply. If it happens to be the most efficient weapon in the narcissist's arsenal, he makes profligate use of it. In other words: if the narcissist cannot obtain adoration, admiration, approval, applause, or any other kind of attention by other means (e.g., intellectually) – he resorts to sex.

He then become a satyr (or a nymphomaniac): indiscriminately engages in sex with multiple partners. His sex partners are considered by him to be objects - sources of Narcissistic Supply. It is through the processes of successful seduction and sexual conquest that the narcissist derives his badly needed narcissistic "fix".

The narcissist is likely to perfect his techniques of courting and regard his sexual exploits as a form of art. He usually exposes this side of him – in great detail – to others, to an audience, expecting to win their approval and admiration. Because the Narcissistic Supply in his case is in the very act of conquest and (what he perceives to be) subordination – the narcissist is forced to hop from one partner to another.

Some narcissists prefer "complicated" situations. If men – they prefer virgins, married women, frigid or lesbian women, etc. The more "difficult" the target – the more rewarding the narcissistic outcome. Such a narcissist may be married, but he does not regard his extra-marital affairs as either immoral or a breach of any explicit or implicit contract between him and his spouse.

He keeps explaining to anyone who cares to listen that his other sexual partners are nothing to him, meaningless, that he is merely taking advantage of them and that they do not constitute a threat and should not be taken seriously by his spouse. In his mind a clear separation exists between the honest "woman of his life" (really, a saint) and the whores that he is having sex with.

With the exception of the meaningful women in his life, he tends to view all females in a bad light. His behaviour, thus, achieves a dual purpose: securing Narcissistic Supply, on the one hand – and re-enacting old, unresolved conflicts and traumas (abandonment by Primary Objects and the Oedipal conflict, for instance).

When inevitably abandoned by his spouse – the narcissist is veritably shocked and hurt. This is the sort of crisis, which might drive him to psychotherapy. Still, deep inside, he feels compelled to continue to pursue precisely the same path. His abandonment is cathartic, purifying. Following a period of deep depression and suicidal ideation – the narcissist is likely to feel cleansed, invigorated, unshackled, ready for the next round of hunting.

But there is another type of narcissist. He also has bouts of sexual hyperactivity in which he trades sexual partners and tends to regard them as objects. However, with him, this is a secondary behaviour. It appears mainly after major narcissistic traumas and crises.

A painful divorce, a devastating personal financial upheaval – and this type of narcissist adopts the view that the "old" (intellectual) solutions do not work anymore. He frantically gropes and searches for new ways to attract attention, to restore his False Ego (=his grandiosity) and to secure a subsistence level of Narcissistic Supply.

Sex is handy and is a great source of the right kind of supply: it is immediate, sexual partners are interchangeable, the solution is comprehensive (it encompasses all the aspects of the narcissist's being), natural, highly charged, adventurous, and pleasurable. Thus, following a life crisis, the cerebral narcissist is likely to be deeply involved in sexual activities – very frequently and almost to the exclusion of all other matters.

However, as the memories of the crisis fade, as the narcissistic wounds heal, as the Narcissistic Cycle re-commences and the balance is restored – this second type of narcissist reveals his true colours. He abruptly loses interest in sex and in all his sexual partners. The frequency of his sexual activities deteriorates from a few times a day – to a few times a year. He reverts to intellectual pursuits, sports, politics, voluntary activities – anything but sex.

The cerebral narcissist renders himself unattractive to his partners by gaining weight, neglecting his body and personal hygiene, not attending to his rotting teeth and crumbling health, and dressing shabbily. This self-inflicted and ostentatious abuse has the effect of bringing sexual and physical intimacy to a screeching halt and forcing his mate or spouse into patterns of behavior and lifestyle alien to her nature: if she is a codependent and fears abandonment she abjures sex altogether (becomes asexual) and if she is not, she is forced into adultery and promiscuity.

This kind of narcissist is afraid of encounters with the opposite sex and is even more afraid of emotional involvement or commitment that he fancies himself prone to develop following a sexual encounter. In general, such a narcissist withdraws not only sexually – but also emotionally. If married – he loses all overt interest in his spouse, sexual or otherwise. He confines himself to his world and makes sure that he is sufficiently busy to preclude any interaction with his nearest (and supposedly dearest).

He becomes completely immersed in "big projects", lifelong plans, a vision, or a cause – all very rewarding narcissistically and all very demanding and time consuming. In such circumstances, sex inevitably becomes an obligation, a necessity, or a maintenance chore reluctantly undertaken to preserve his sources of supply (his family or household).

The cerebral narcissist does not enjoy sex and by far prefers masturbation or "objective", emotionless sex, like going to prostitutes. Actually, he uses his mate or spouse as an "alibi", a shield against the attentions of other women, an insurance policy which preserves his virile image while making it socially and morally commendable for him to avoid any intimate or sexual contact with others.

Ostentatiously ignoring women other than his wife (a form of aggression I call "ostentatious fidelity") he feels righteous in saying: "I am a faithful husband". At the same time, he feels hostility towards his spouse for ostensibly preventing him from freely expressing his sexuality, for isolating him from carnal pleasures.

The narcissist's thwarted logic goes something like this: "I am married/attached to this woman. Therefore, I am not allowed to be in any form of contact with other women which might be interpreted as more than casual or businesslike. This is why I refrain from having anything to do with women – because I am being faithful, as opposed to most other immoral men.

However, I do not like this situation. I envy my free peers. They can have as much sex and romance as they want to – while I am confined to this marriage, chained by my wife, my freedom curbed. I am angry at her and I will punish her by abstaining from having sex with her."

Thus frustrated, the narcissist minimises all manner of intercourse with his close circle (spouse, children, parents, siblings, very intimate friends): sexual, verbal, or emotional. He limits himself to the rawest exchanges of information and isolates himself socially.

His reclusion insures against a future hurt and avoids the intimacy that he so dreads. But, again, this way he also secures abandonment and the replay of old, unresolved, conflicts. Finally, he really is left alone by everyone, with no Secondary Sources of Supply.

In his quest to find new sources, he again embarks on ego-mending bouts of sex, followed by the selection of a spouse or a mate (a Secondary Narcissistic Supply Source). Then the cycle re-commence: a sharp drop in sexual activity, emotional absence and cruel detachment leading to abandonment.

The second type of narcissist is mostly sexually loyal to his spouse. He alternates between what appears to be hyper-sexuality and asexuality (really, forcefully repressed sexuality). In the second phase, he feels no sexual urges, bar the most basic. He is, therefore, not compelled to "cheat" upon his mate, betray her, or violate the marital vows. He is much more interested in preventing a worrisome dwindling of the kind of Narcissistic Supply that really matters. Sex, he says to himself, contentedly, is for those who can do no better.

This is not affected abstinence or ostentatious celibacy, though. The repressed libido all but vanishes and, in this sense, the cerebral narcissist is intermittently asexual, albeit never sex-averse. Many cerebral narcissists are also schizoids and avoid gratuitous social contact as they do sexual congress.

Both types of avoidance have similar psychodynamic roots: fear of loss of control and of escalation as others are seen to dictate the frequency, intensity, and details of sexual or social encounters (the cerebral narcissist may end up being bored out of his mind, or compelled to participate in activities he would rather avoid) and the perception of sex and gregariousness as breaches of personal boundaries: sexual or social partners know no limits and are liable to be all over the cerebral narcissist if he allows them, driving him to defend his privacy aggressively and unpleasantly.

Paradoxically, once forced into the action, the cerebral narcissist finds both sex and socializing to be pleasurable and enjoyable activities. But, he simply lacks the willpower and predilection to initiate or to participate in these interactions unless absolutely coerced to.

Somatic narcissists tend to verbal exhibitionism. They tend to brag in graphic details about their conquests and exploits. In extreme cases, they might introduce "live witnesses" and revert to total, classical exhibitionism. This sits well with their tendency to "objectify" their sexual partners, to engage in emotionally-neutral sex (group sex, for instance) and to indulge in autoerotic sex.

The exhibitionist sees himself reflected in the eyes of the beholders. This constitutes the main sexual stimulus, this is what turns him on. This outside "look" is also what defines the narcissist. There is bound to be a connection. One (the exhibitionist) may be the culmination, the "pure case" of the other (the narcissist).

Narcissists cheat on their spouses, commit adultery and have extramarital affairs and liaisons for a variety of reasons which reflect disparate psychodynamic processes:

1. In the quest for narcissistic supply, the somatic narcissist resorts to serial sexual conquests.

2. Narcissists are easily bored (they have a low boredom threshold) and they have a low tolerance for boredom. Sexual dalliances alleviate this nagging and frustrating ennui.

3. Narcissists maintain an island and focus of stability in their life, but all the other dimensions of their existence are chaotic, unstable, and unpredictable. This "twister" formation serves many emotional needs which I expound upon elsewhere. Thus, a narcissist may be a model employee and pursue a career path over decades even as he cheats on his wife and fritters their savings away.

4. Narcissists feel superior and important and so entitled to be above the law and to engage in behaviors that are frowned upon and considered socially unacceptable in others. They reject and vehemently resent all limitations and conditions placed upon them by their partners. They act on their impulses and desires unencumbered by social conventions and strictures.

5. Marriage, monogamy, and child-bearing and rearing are common activities that characterize the average person. The narcissist feels robbed of his uniqueness by these pursuits and coerced into the relationship and into roles - such as a husband and a father - that reduce him to the lowest of common denominators. This narcissistic injury leads him to rebel and reassert his superiority and specialness by maintaining extramarital affairs.

6. Narcissists are control freaks. Having a relationship implies a give-and-take and a train of compromises which the narcissist acutely interprets to mean a loss of control over his life. To reassert control, the narcissist initiates other relationships in which he dictates the terms of engagement (love affairs).

7. Narcissists are terrified of intimacy. Their behavior is best characterized as an approach-avoidance repetition complex. Adultery is an excellent tool in the attempt to retard intimacy and resort to a less threatening mode of interaction.

Narcissists typically claim that they have cheated in order to "put the spark back into the relationship (with the spouse or primary intimate partner.)" Of course, how exactly an act of betrayal and faithlessness can rekindle the ambers of a relationship founded initially on trust and sexual and emotional exclusivity is left conveniently unsaid.

In the wake of an affair, the narcissist possesses the perfect alibi: if he does try to revive his sex life with his spouse and fails, he can proudly say: "I left no stone unturned, I even went as far as cheating on my partner – all in order to resurrect our bond!" If he doesn't try to reanimate his sex life with his spouse, he turns it around and says: "This is proof that the relationship was doomed to start with and what I did was, therefore, not cheating. I was actually FORCED to seek sexual and emotional alternatives by the dead weight of this relationship."

Sexual Fantasies of Narcissists and Psychopaths

Click HERE to Watch the Video

Inevitably, the sexual fantasy life of narcissists and psychopaths reflects their psychodynamic landscape: their fear of intimacy, misogyny, control freakiness, auto-eroticism, latent sadism and masochism, problems of gender identity, and various sexual paraphilias.

Fantasies which reflect a **fear of intimacy** involve the aggressive or violent objectification of a faceless, nameless, and sometimes sexless person, often in impersonal, alien or foreign settings (example: narratives of rape.) These usually coalesce with **misogynistic erotic storylines** in which females are humiliated, coerced into hurtful submission, and subjected to violation and degradation by one or many. Where **sadism-masochism,** homosexuality, or sexual paraphilias such as pedophilia are present, they are injected into the fantasy and colour its composition and progression.

In his fantasies, the narcissist or psychopath is always in unmitigated **control** of the environment. The assemblages of bodies and limbs which populate his daydreams – his body included - are minutely choreographed to yield maximum titillation. He is like an exhibitionistic and voyeuristic porn director with an endless supply of well-endowed actors either cowed into compliance or craving it. Naturally, the narcissist's fantasies are devoid of any performance anxiety or of the need to reciprocate in the sex act by pleasing his anonymous and robotic partners.

Such imaginarium invariably leads to acts of self-stimulation, the ultimate manifestations of **auto-eroticism**. Even when the narcissist incorporates his real-life partner in his fantasies, he is bound to treat her as a mere prop, a body to masturbate with, in, or on, or an object to be "defiled" in acts such as group sex, swinging (wife-swapping), or outright sexual deviance (examples: urophilia, or coprophilia.) This crude and overt denigration serves to render her a "slut", or a "whore" in his mind, the kind of woman with whom he can have lustful, emotion-free sex. He reserves love, involvement, and intimacy to sexless "madonna"-type, sexually inaccessible or unattainable women, such as his mother.

The somatic narcissist's and psychopath's sexual promiscuity emerges from underlying problems in **gender identity**. Many of them are closet bisexuals, cross-dressers, and prone to paraphilias such as pedophilia, fetishism, and sexual sadism or masochism. Some of them try to act out their fantasies and get their partners to assume roles commensurate with their propensities and predilections, however outlandish, illegal, or extreme.

A useful test to tell apart healthy sexual fantasies from narcissistic ones is to pose the question: would you be equally satisfied having sex with a sophisticated inflatable robotic doll as with a flesh and blood partner? If the answer is "yes", then, in all likelihood, we are dealing with a narcissist or a psychopath.

Yet, these glimpses into the thwarted and the demented rarely go down well with their significant others. The narcissist's self-exposure often elicits reactions of horror, repulsion, and estrangement. No wonder most narcissists don't even bother to share their fantasies with their "loved" ones. The cerebral narcissist merely retreats to sexual abstinence punctuated by compulsive, porn-fuelled masturbation. The somatic narcissist compulsively hunts for new feminine prey to sacrifice on the insatiable altar of his False Self.

Sin of self-love possesseth all mine eye
And all my soul and all my every part;
And for this sin there is no remedy,
It is so grounded inward in my heart.
Methinks no face so gracious is as mine,
No shape so true, no truth of such account;
And for myself mine own worth do define,
As I all other in all worths surmount.
But when my glass shows me myself indeed,
Beated and chopp'd with tann'd antiquity,
Mine own self-love quite contrary I read;
Self so self-loving were iniquity.
'Tis thee, myself, that for myself I praise,
Painting my age with beauty of thy days.

(Sonnet 62, William Shakespeare)

The Narcissist and His Family

At first, the narcissist treats newborn siblings and children as competitors for scarce narcissistic supply.

Gradually, though, he converts them into sources of attention and adulation (at this phase, incest is a distinct danger)

As they grow up and become more discerning, judgmental, and critical, the narcissist regains his erstwhile hostility towards his offspring.

Question:

Is there a "typical" relationship between the narcissist and his family?

Answer:

We are all members of a few families in our lifetime: the one that we are born to and the one(s) that we create. We all transfer hurts, attitudes, fears, hopes and desires – a whole emotional baggage – from the former to the latter. The narcissist is no exception.

The narcissist has a dichotomous view of humanity: humans are either Sources of Narcissistic Supply (and, then, idealised and over-valued) or do not fulfil this function (and, therefore, are valueless, devalued). The narcissist gets all the love that he needs from himself. From the outside he needs approval, affirmation, admiration, adoration, attention – in other words, externalised Ego boundary functions.

He does not require – nor does he seek – his parents' or his siblings' love, or to be loved by his children. He casts them as the audience in the theatre of his inflated grandiosity. He wishes to impress them, shock them, threaten them, infuse them with awe, inspire them, attract their attention, subjugate them, or manipulate them.

He emulates and simulates an entire range of emotions and employs every means to achieve these effects. He lies (narcissists are pathological liars – their very self is a false one). He acts the pitiful, or, its opposite, the resilient and reliable. He stuns and shines with outstanding intellectual, or physical capacities and achievements, or behavior patterns appreciated by the members of the family. When confronted with (younger) siblings or with his own children, the narcissist is likely to go through three phases:

At first, he perceives his offspring or siblings as a threat to his Narcissistic Supply, such as the attention of his spouse, or mother, as the case may be. They intrude on his turf and invade the Pathological Narcissistic Space. The narcissist does his best to belittle them, hurt (even physically) and humiliate them and then, when these reactions prove ineffective or counter productive, he retreats into an imaginary world of omnipotence. A period of emotional absence and detachment ensues.

His aggression having failed to elicit Narcissistic Supply, the narcissist proceeds to indulge himself in daydreaming, delusions of grandeur, planning of future coups, nostalgia and hurt (the Lost Paradise Syndrome). The narcissist reacts this way to the birth of his children or to the introduction of new foci of attention to the family cell (even to a new pet!).

Whomever the narcissist perceives to be in competition for scarce Narcissistic Supply is relegated to the role of the enemy. Where the uninhibited expression of the aggression and hostility aroused by this predicament is illegitimate or impossible – the narcissist prefers to stay away. Rather than attack his offspring or siblings, he sometimes immediately disconnects, detaches himself emotionally, becomes cold and uninterested, or directs transformed anger at his mate or at his parents (the more "legitimate" targets).

Other narcissists see the opportunity in the "mishap". They seek to manipulate their parents (or their mate) by "taking over" the newcomer. Such narcissists monopolise their siblings or their newborn children. This way, indirectly, they benefit from the attention directed at the infants. The sibling or offspring become vicarious sources of Narcissistic Supply and proxies for the narcissist.

An example: by being closely identified with his offspring, a narcissistic father secures the grateful admiration of the mother ("What an outstanding father/brother he is"). He also assumes part of or all the credit for baby's/sibling's achievements. This is a process of annexation and assimilation of the other, a strategy that the narcissist makes use of in most of his relationships.

As siblings or progeny grow older, the narcissist begins to see their potential to be edifying, reliable and satisfactory Sources of Narcissistic Supply. His attitude, then, is completely transformed. The former threats have now become promising potentials. He cultivates those whom he trusts to be the most rewarding. He encourages them to idolise him, to adore him, to be awed by him, to admire his deeds and capabilities, to learn to blindly trust and obey him, in short to surrender to his charisma and to become submerged in his follies-de-grandeur.

It is at this stage that the risk of child abuse - from emotional incest and up to and including outright incest - is heightened. The narcissist is auto-erotic. He is the preferred object of his own sexual attraction. His siblings and his children share his genetic material. Molesting or having intercourse with them is as close as the narcissist gets to having sex with himself.

Moreover, the narcissist perceives sex in terms of annexation. The partner is "assimilated" and becomes an extension of the narcissist, a fully controlled and manipulated object. Sex, to the narcissist, is the ultimate act of depersonalization and objectification of the other. He actually masturbates with other people's bodies.

Minors pose little danger of criticizing the narcissist or confronting him. They are perfect, malleable and abundant sources of Narcissistic Supply. The narcissist derives gratification from having coital relations with adulating, physically and mentally inferior, inexperienced and dependent "bodies".

These roles – allocated to them explicitly and demandingly or implicitly and perniciously by the narcissist – are best fulfilled by ones whose mind is not yet fully formed and independent. The older the siblings or offspring, the more they become critical, even judgemental, of the narcissist. They are better able to put into context and perspective his actions, to question his motives, to anticipate his moves.

As they mature, they often refuse to continue to play the mindless pawns in his chess game. They hold grudges against him for what he has done to them in the past, when they were less capable of resistance. They can gauge his true stature, talents and achievements – which, usually, lag far behind the claims that he makes.

This brings the narcissist a full cycle back to the first phase. Again, he perceives his siblings or sons/daughters as threats. He quickly becomes disillusioned and devaluing. He loses all interest, becomes emotionally remote, absent and cold, rejects any effort to communicate with him, citing life pressures and the preciousness and scarceness of his time.

He feels burdened, cornered, besieged, suffocated, and claustrophobic. He wants to get away, to abandon his commitments to people who have become totally useless (or even damaging) to him. He does not understand why he has to support them, or to suffer their company and he believes himself to have been deliberately and ruthlessly trapped.

He rebels either passively-aggressively (by refusing to act or by intentionally sabotaging the relationships) or actively (by being overly critical, aggressive, unpleasant, verbally and psychologically abusive and so on). Slowly – to justify his acts to himself – he gets immersed in conspiracy theories with clear paranoid hues.

To his mind, the members of the family conspire against him, seek to belittle or humiliate or subordinate him, do not understand him, or stymie his growth. The narcissist usually finally gets what he wants and the family that he has created disintegrates to his great sorrow (due to the loss of the Narcissistic Space) – but also to his great relief and surprise (how could they have let go someone as unique as he?).

This is the cycle: the narcissist feels threatened by arrival of new family members – he tries to assimilate or annex of siblings or offspring – he obtains Narcissistic Supply from them – he overvalues and idealizes these newfound sources – as sources grow older and independent, they adopt anti narcissistic behaviours – the narcissist devalues them – the narcissist feels stifled and trapped – the narcissist becomes paranoid – the narcissist rebels and the family disintegrates.

This cycle characterises not only the family life of the narcissist. It is to be found in other realms of his life (his career, for instance). At work, the narcissist, initially, feels threatened (no one knows him, he is a nobody). Then, he develops a circle of admirers, cronies and friends which he "nurtures and cultivates" in order to obtain Narcissistic Supply from them. He overvalues them (to him, they are the brightest, the most loyal, with the biggest chances to climb the corporate ladder and other superlatives).

But following some anti-narcissistic behaviours on their part (a critical remark, a disagreement, a refusal, however polite) – the narcissist devalues all these previously idealized individuals. Now that they have dared oppose him - they are judged by him to be stupid, cowardly, lacking in ambition, skills and talents, common (the worst expletive in the narcissist's vocabulary), with an unspectacular career ahead of them.

The narcissist feels that he is misallocating his scarce and invaluable resources (for instance, his time). He feels besieged and suffocated. He rebels and erupts in a serious of self-defeating and self-destructive behaviours, which lead to the disintegration of his life.

Doomed to build and ruin, attach and detach, appreciate and depreciate, the narcissist is predictable in his "death wish". What sets him apart from other suicidal types is that his wish is granted to him in small, tormenting doses throughout his anguished life.

Appendix: Custody and Visitation

Click HERE to Watch the Video

A parent diagnosed with full-fledged Narcissistic Personality Disorder (NPD) should be denied custody and be granted only restricted rights of visitation under supervision.

Narcissists accord the same treatment to children and adults. They regard both as sources of narcissistic supply, mere instruments of gratification - idealize them at first and then devalue them in favour of alternative, safer and more subservient, sources. Such treatment is traumatic and can have long-lasting emotional effects.

The narcissist's inability to acknowledge and abide by the personal boundaries set by others puts the child at heightened risk of abuse - verbal, emotional, physical, and, often, sexual. His possessiveness and panoply of indiscriminate negative emotions - transformations of aggression, such as rage and envy - hinder his ability to act as a "good enough" parent. His propensities for reckless behaviour, substance abuse, and sexual deviance endanger the child's welfare, or even his or her life.

The Unstable Narcissist

Dependent on and addicted to fluctuating narcissistic supply, the narcissist's life and mood are volatile.

The classic narcissist maintains an island of stability in his life while the other dimensions of his existence wallow in chaos and unpredictability.

The borderline narcissist reacts to instability in one area of his life by introducing chaos into all the others.

Question:

Is the narcissist characterised by simultaneous instabilities in all the important aspects of his life?

Answer:

The narcissist is a person who derives his Ego (and Ego functions) from other people's reactions to an image he invents and projects, called the False Self (Narcissistic Supply). Since no absolute control over the quantity and quality of Narcissistic Supply is possible – it is bound to fluctuate – the narcissist's view of himself and of his world is correspondingly and equally volatile. As "public opinion" ebbs and flows, so do the narcissist's self-confidence, self-esteem, sense of self-worth, or, in other words, so does his Self. Even the narcissist's convictions are subject to a never-ending process of vetting by others.

The narcissistic personality is unstable in each and every one of its dimensions. It is the ultimate hybrid: rigidly amorphous, devoutly flexible, reliant for its sustenance on the opinion of people, whom the narcissist undervalues. A large part of this instability is subsumed under the Emotional Involvement Prevention Measures (EIPM) that I describe in the Essay. The narcissist's lability is so ubiquitous and so dominant – that it might well be described as the ***ONLY*** stable feature of his personality.

The narcissist does everything with one goal in mind: to attract Narcissistic Supply (attention).

An example of this kind of behaviour:

The narcissist may study a given subject diligently and in great depth in order to impress people later with this newly acquired erudition. But, having served its purpose, the narcissist lets the knowledge thus acquired evaporate. The narcissist maintains a sort of a "short-term" cell or warehouse where he stores whatever may come handy in the pursuit of Narcissistic Supply. But he is almost never really interested in what he does, studies, and experiences.

From the outside, this might be perceived as instability. But think about it this way: the narcissist is constantly preparing for life's "exams" and feels that he is on a permanent trial. It is common to forget material studied only in preparation for an exam or for a court appearance.

Short-term memory is perfectly normal. What sets the narcissist apart is the fact that, with him, this short-termism is a ***CONSTANT*** state of affairs and affects ***ALL*** his functions, not only those directly related to learning, or to emotions, or to experience, or to any single dimension of his life.

Thus, the narcissist learns, remembers and forgets not in line with his real interests or hobbies, he loves and hates not the real subjects of his emotions but one dimensional, utilitarian, cartoons constructed by him. He judges, praises and condemns – all from the narrowest possible point of view: the potential to extract Narcissistic Supply.

He asks not what he can do with the world and in it – but what can the world do for him as far as Narcissistic Supply goes. He falls in and out of love with people, workplaces, residences, vocations, hobbies, interests – because they seem to be able to provide more or less Narcissistic Supply and for no other reason.

Still, narcissists belong to two broad categories: the "compensatory stability" and the "enhancing instability" types.

I. Compensatory Stability ("Classic") Narcissists

These narcissists isolate one or more (but never most) aspects of their lives and "make these aspect/s stable". They do not really invest themselves in it. This stability is maintained by artificial means: money, celebrity, power, fear. A typical example is a narcissist who changes numerous workplaces, a few careers, a myriad of hobbies, value systems or faiths. At the same time, he maintains (preserves) a relationship with a single woman (and even remains faithful to her). She is his "island of stability". To fulfil this role, she just needs to be there for him physically.

The narcissist is dependent upon "his" woman to maintain the stability lacking in all other areas of his life (to compensate for his instability). Yet, emotional closeness is bound to threaten the narcissist. Thus, he is likely to distance himself from her and to remain detached and indifferent to most of her needs.

Despite this cruel emotional treatment, the narcissist considers her to be a point of exit, a form of sustenance, a fountain of empowerment. This mismatch between what he wishes to receive and what he is able to give, the narcissist prefers to deny, repress and bury deep in his unconscious.

This is why he is always shocked and devastated to learn of his wife's estrangement, infidelity, or intentions to divorce him. Possessed of no emotional depth, being completely one track minded – he cannot fathom the needs of others. In other words, he cannot empathise.

Another – even more common – case is the "career narcissist". This narcissist marries, divorces and remarries with dizzying speed. Everything in his life is in constant flux: friends, emotions, judgements, values, beliefs, place of residence, affiliations, hobbies. Everything, that is, except his work.

His career is the island of compensating stability in his otherwise mercurial existence. This kind of narcissist is dogged by unmitigated ambition and devotion. He perseveres in one workplace or one job, patiently, persistently and blindly climbing up the corporate ladder and treading the career path. In his pursuit of job fulfilment and achievements, the narcissist is ruthless and unscrupulous – and, very often, successful.

II. Enhancing Instability ("Borderline") Narcissist

The other kind of narcissist enhances instability in one aspect or dimension of his life – by introducing instability in others. Thus, if such a narcissist resigns (or, more likely, is made redundant) – he also relocates to another city or country. If he divorces, he is also likely to resign his job.

This added instability gives this type of narcissist the feeling that all the dimensions of his life are changing simultaneously, that he is being "unshackled", that a transformation is in progress. This, of course, is an illusion. Those who know the narcissist, no longer trust his frequent "conversions", "decisions", "crises", "transformations", "developments" and "periods". They see through his pretensions, protestations, and solemn declarations into the core of his instability. They know that he is not to be relied upon. They know that with narcissists, temporariness is the only permanence.

Narcissists hate routine. When a narcissist finds himself doing the same things over and over again, he gets depressed. He oversleeps, over-eats, over-drinks and, in general, engages in addictive, impulsive, reckless, and compulsive behaviours. This is his way of re-introducing risk and excitement into what he (emotionally) perceives to be a barren life.

The problem is that even the most exciting and varied existence becomes routine after a while. Living in the same country or apartment, meeting the same people, doing essentially the same things (even with changing content) – all "qualify", in the eyes of the narcissist, as stultifying rote.

The narcissist <u>feels entitled</u>. He feels it is his right – due to his intellectual or physical superiority – to lead a thrilling, rewarding, kaleidoscopic life. He wants to force life itself, or at least people around him, to yield to his wishes and needs, supreme among them the need for stimulating variety.

This rejection of <u>habit</u> is part of a larger pattern of aggressive entitlement. The narcissist feels that the very existence of a sublime intellect (such as his) warrants concessions and allowances by others.

Thus, standing in line is a waste of time better spent pursuing knowledge, inventing and creating. The narcissist should avail himself of the best medical treatment proffered by the most prominent medical authorities – lest the precious asset that is the narcissist is lost to Mankind. He should not be bothered with trivial pursuits – these lowly functions are best assigned to the less gifted. The devil is in paying precious attention to detail.

Entitlement is sometimes justified in a Picasso or an Einstein. But few narcissists are either. Their achievements are grotesquely incommensurate with their overwhelming sense of entitlement and with their grandiose self-image.

Of course, this overpowering sense of superiority often serves to mask and compensate for a cancerous complex of inferiority. Moreover, the narcissist infects others with his projected grandiosity and their feedback constitutes the edifice upon which he constructs his self-esteem. He regulates his sense of self worth by rigidly insisting that he is above the madding crowd while deriving his Narcissistic Supply from the very people he holds in deep contempt.

But there is a second angle to this abhorrence of the predictable. Narcissists employ a host of <u>Emotional Involvement Prevention Measures (EIPM's)</u>. Despising routine and avoiding it is one of these mechanisms. Their function is to prevent the narcissist from getting emotionally involved and, subsequently, hurt.

Their application results in an "approach-avoidance repetition complex". The narcissist, fearing and loathing intimacy, stability and security – yet craving them – approaches and then avoids significant others or important tasks in a rapid succession of apparently inconsistent and disconnected cycles.

Narcissist of Substance vs. Narcissist of Appearances

Click <u>HERE</u> to Watch the Video

Why do some narcissists end up being over-achievers, pillars of the community, and accomplished professionals - while their brethren fade into obscurity, having done little of note with their lives?

There seem to be two types of narcissists: those who derive ample <u>narcissistic supply</u> from mere appearances and those whose narcissistic supply consists of doing substantial deeds, of acting as change-agents, of making a difference, and of creating and producing things of value. The former aim for celebrity (defined as "being famous for being famous"), the latter aim for careers in the limelight.

The celebrity narcissist has a short attention span. He rapidly cycles between the idealization and devaluation of ideas, ventures, places, and people. This renders him unfit for team work. Though energetic and manic, he is indolent: he prefers the path of least resistance and adheres to shoddy standards of production. His lack of work ethic can partly be attributed to his overpowering sense of entitlement and to his magical thinking, both of which give rise to unrealistic expectations of effortless outcomes.

The life of the celebrity narcissist is chaotic and characterized by inconsistency and by a dire lack of long-term planning and commitment. He is not really interested in people (except in their roles as instruments of instant gratification and sources of narcissistic supply). His learning and affected erudition are designed solely to impress and are, therefore, shallow and anecdotal. His actions are not geared towards creating works of lasting value, effecting change, or making a difference. All he cares about is attention: provoking and garnering it in copious quantities. The celebrity narcissist is, therefore, not above confabulating, plagiarizing, and otherwise using short-cuts to obtain his fix.

The other strain of narcissist, the career narcissist, is very concerned with leaving his mark and stamp on the world. He feels a calling, often of cosmic significance. He is busy reforming his environment, transforming his milieu, making a difference, and producing and creating an oeuvre of standing value. His is a grandiose idée fixe which he cathexes. To scale these lofty self-imputed peaks and to realize his goals, the career narcissist acts with unswerving passion and commitment. He plans and inexorably and ruthlessly implements his schemes and stratagems, a workaholic in pursuit of glory and fame.

The career narcissist does not recoil from cutting the odd corner, proffering the occasional confabulation, or absconding with the fruits of someone else's labor. But while these amount to the entire arsenal and the exclusive modus operandi of the celebrity narcissist, they are auxiliary as far as the career narcissist is concerned. His main weapon is toil.

The career narcissist is a natural-born leader. When not a guru at the center of a cult, he operates as the first among equals in a team. This is where the differences between the celebrity narcissist and the career narcissist are most pronounced: the relationships maintained by the former are manipulative, exploitative, and ephemeral. The career narcissist, by comparison, is willing and able to negotiate, compromise, give-and-take, motivate others, induce loyalty, forge alliances and coalitions and benefit from these in the long-term. It is this capacity to network that guarantees him a place in the common memory and an abiding reputation among his peers.

The Extra-Marital Narcissist

Somatic narcissists use sexual conquests and ostentatious sexual prowess as narcissistic supply. Hence their serial extramarital affairs, cheating, and infidelity.

If you can't or won't leave him, promulgate clear rules and sanctions and penalties when these are violated. Be fair, but merciless.

Question:

My husband has a liaison with another woman. He has been diagnosed as suffering from a Narcissistic Personality Disorder. What should I do?

Answer:

Narcissists are people who fail to maintain a stable sense of self-worth. Very often somatic narcissists (narcissistic who use their bodies and their sexuality to secure Narcissistic Supply) tend to get involved in extra-marital affairs. The new "conquests" sustain their grandiose fantasies and their distorted and unrealistic self-image.

It is, therefore, nigh impossible to alter this particular behaviour of a somatic narcissist. Sexual interactions serve as a constant, reliable, easy to obtain Source of Narcissistic Supply. It is the only source of such supply if the narcissist is not cerebral (=does not rely on his intellect, intelligence, or professional achievements for Narcissistic Supply).

You should set up rigid, strict and **VERY WELL DEFINED** rules of engagement. Ideally, all contacts between your spouse and his lover should be immediately and irrevocably severed. But this is usually too much to ask for. So, you should make crystal clear when is she allowed to call, whether she is allowed to write to him at all and in which circumstances, what are the subjects she is allowed to broach in her correspondence and phone calls, when is he allowed to see her and what other modes of interaction are permissible.

CLEAR AND PAINFUL SANCTIONS must be defined in case the above rules are violated. Both rules and sanctions **MUST BE APPLIED RIGOROUSLY AND MERCILESSLY** and **MUST BE SET IN WRITING IN UNEQUIVOCAL TERMS.**

The problem is that the narcissist never really separates from his Sources of Narcissistic Supply until and unless they cease to be ones. Narcissists never really say good-bye. His lover is likely to still have an emotional hold on him. Your husband must first have his day of reckoning.

Help him by telling him what will be the price that he stands to pay if he does not obey the rules and sanctions you have agreed on. Tell him that you cannot live like this any longer. That if he does not get rid of this presence – of the echoes of his past, really – he will be squandering his present, he will be forfeiting you. Don't be afraid to lose him. If he prefers this woman to you – it is important for you to know it. If he prefers you to her – your nightmare is over.

If you insist on staying with him – you must also be prepared to serve as a Source of Narcissistic Supply, an alternative to the supply provided by his former lover. You must brace yourself: serving as a Narcissistic Supply Source is an onerous task, a full time job and a very ungrateful one at that. The narcissist's thirst for adulation, admiration, worship, approval, and attention can never by quenched. It is a Sisyphean, mind-numbing effort, which heralds only additional demands and disgruntled, critical, humiliating tirades by the narcissist.

That you are afraid to confront reality is normal. You are afraid to set clear alternatives. You are afraid that he will leave you. You are afraid that he will prefer her to you. ***AND YOU MAY WELL BE RIGHT.*** But if this is the case and you go on living with him and tormenting yourself – it is unhealthy.

If you have find it difficult to confront the fact that it is all over between you, that your relationship is an empty shell, that your husband is with another woman – do not hesitate to seek help from professionals and non-professionals alike. But do not let this situation fester into psychological gangrene. Amputate now while you can.

Narcissistic Couples and Narcissistic Types: The Double Reflection

Two narcissists of the same type (somatic, cerebral, inverted) are bound to be at each other's throat in no time.

Two narcissists of different types can make each other very happy indeed as serve as each other's perfect sources of narcissistic supply.

Question:

Can two narcissists establish a long-term, stable relationship?

Answer:

Two narcissists of the same type (somatic, cerebral, classic, compensatory, inverted, etc.) cannot maintain a stable, long-term full-fledged, and functional relationship.

There are two types of narcissists: the somatic narcissist and the cerebral narcissist. The somatic type relies on his body and sexuality as Sources of Narcissistic Supply. The cerebral narcissist uses his intellect, his intelligence and his professional achievements to obtain the same.

Narcissists are either predominantly cerebral or overwhelmingly somatic. In other words, they either generate their Narcissistic Supply by using their bodies or by flaunting their minds.

The somatic narcissist flashes his sexual conquests, parades his possessions, puts his muscles on ostentatious display, brags about his physical aesthetics or sexual prowess or exploits, is often a health freak and a hypochondriac. The cerebral narcissist is a know-it-all, haughty and intelligent "computer". He uses his awesome intellect, or knowledge (real or pretended) to secure adoration, adulation and admiration. To him, his body and its maintenance are a burden and a distraction.

Both types are autoerotic (psychosexually in love with themselves, with their bodies or with their brains). Both types prefer masturbation to adult, mature, interactive, multi-dimensional and emotion-laden sex.

The cerebral narcissist is often celibate (even when he has a girlfriend or a spouse). He prefers pornography and sexual auto-stimulation to the real thing. The cerebral narcissist is sometimes a latent (hidden, not yet outed) homosexual.

The somatic narcissist uses other people's bodies to masturbate. Sex with him – pyrotechnics and acrobatics aside – is likely to be an impersonal and emotionally alienating and draining experience. The partner is often treated as an object, an extension of the somatic narcissist, a toy, a warm and pulsating vibrator.

It is a mistake to assume type-constancy. In other words, all narcissists are both cerebral and somatic. In each narcissist, one of the types is dominant. So, the narcissist is either largely cerebral – or dominantly somatic. But the other, recessive (manifested less frequently) type, is there. It is lurking, waiting to erupt. The narcissist swings between his dominant type and his recessive type which manifests mainly after a major narcissistic injury or life crisis.

The cerebral narcissist brandishes his brainpower, exhibits his intellectual achievements, basks in the attention given to his mind and to its products. He hates his body and neglects it. It is a nuisance, a burden, a derided appendix, an inconvenience, a punishment. The cerebral narcissist is asexual (rarely has sex, often years apart). He masturbates regularly and very mechanically. His fantasies are homosexual or paedophiliac or tend to objectify his partner (rape, group sex). He stays away from women because he perceives them to be ruthless predators who are out to consume him.

The cerebral narcissist typically goes through a few major life crises. He gets divorced, goes bankrupt, does time in prison, is threatened, harassed and stalked, is often devalued, betrayed, denigrated and insulted. He is prone to all manner of chronic illnesses.

Invariably, following every life crisis, the somatic narcissist in him takes over. The cerebral narcissist suddenly becomes a lascivious lecher. When this happens, he maintains a few relationships – replete with abundant and addictive sex – going simultaneously. He sometimes participates in and initiates group sex and mass orgies. He exercises, loses weight and hones his body into an irresistible proposition.

This outburst of unrestrained, primordial lust wanes in a few months and he settles back into his cerebral ways. No sex, no women, no body.

These total reversals of character stun his mates. His girlfriend or spouse finds it impossible to digest this eerie transformation from the gregarious, darkly handsome, well-built and sexually insatiable person that swept her off her feet – to the bodiless, bookwormish hermit with not an inkling of interest in either sex or other carnal pleasures.

The cerebral narcissist misses his somatic half, but finding a balance is a doomed quest. The satyre that is the somatic narcissist is forever trapped in the intellectual cage of the cerebral one, the Brain.

Thus, if both members of the couple are cerebral narcissists, for instance if both of them are scholars – the resulting competition prevents them from serving as ample Sources of Narcissistic Supply to each other. Finally the mutual admiration society crumbles.

Consumed by the pursuit of their own narcissistic gratification, they have no time or energy or will left to cater to the narcissistic needs of their partner. Moreover, the partner is perceived as a dangerous and vicious contender for a scarce resource: Sources of Narcissistic Supply. This may be less true if the two narcissists work in totally unrelated academic or intellectual fields.

But if the narcissists involved are of different types, if one of them is cerebral and the other one somatic, a long-term partnership based on the mutual provision of Narcissistic Supply can definitely survive.

Example: if one of the narcissists is somatic (uses his/her body as a source of narcissistic gratification) and the other one cerebral (uses his intellect or his professional achievements as such a source), there is nothing to destabilise such collaboration. It is even potentially emotionally rewarding.

The relationship between these two narcissists resembles the one that exists between an artist and his art or or a collector and his collection. This can and does change, of course, as the narcissists involved grow older, flabbier and less agile intellectually. The somatic narcissist is also prone to multiple sexual relationships and encounters intended to support his somatic and sexual self-image. These may subject the relationship to fracturing strains. But, all in all, a stable and enduring relationship can – and often does – develop between dissimilar narcissists.

The Two Loves of the Narcissist

Narcissists "love" their spouses or other significant others – as long as they continue to reliably provide them with Narcissistic Supply (in one word, with attention). Inevitably, they regard others as mere "sources", objects, or functions. Lacking empathy and emotional maturity, the narcissist's love is pathological. But the precise locus of the pathology depends on the narcissist's stability or instability in different parts of his life.

From "The Unstable Narcissist":

(I have omitted below large sections. For a more elaborate treatment, please read the FAQ itself.)

"Narcissists belong to two broad categories: the 'compensatory stability' and the 'enhancing instability' types.

I. Compensatory Stability ('Classic') Narcissists

These narcissists isolate one or more (but never most) aspects of their lives and 'make these aspect/s stable'. They do not really invest themselves in it. The stability is maintained by artificial means: money, celebrity, power, fear. A typical example is a narcissist who changes numerous workplaces, a few careers, a myriad of hobbies, value systems or faiths. At the same time, he maintains (preserves) a relationship with a single woman (and even remains faithful to her). She is his 'island of stability'. To fulfil this role, she just needs to be there physically.

The narcissist is dependent upon 'his' woman to maintain the stability lacking in all other areas of his life (to compensate for his instability). Yet, emotional closeness is bound to threaten the narcissist. Thus, he is likely to distance himself from her and to remain detached and indifferent to most of her needs. Despite this cruel emotional treatment, the narcissist considers her to be a point of exit, a form of sustenance, a fountain of empowerment. This mismatch between what he wishes to receive and what he is able to give, the narcissist prefers to deny, repress and bury deep in his unconscious. This is why he is always shocked and devastated to learn of his wife's estrangement, infidelity, or divorce intentions. Possessed of no emotional depth, being completely one track minded – he cannot fathom the needs of others. In other words, he cannot empathise.

II. Enhancing Instability ('Borderline') Narcissist

The other kind of narcissist enhances instability in one aspect or dimension of his life – by introducing instability in others. Thus, if such a narcissist resigns (or, more likely, is made redundant) – he also relocates to another city or country. If he divorces, he is also likely to resign his job. This added instability gives these narcissists the feeling that all the dimensions of their life are changing simultaneously, that they are being 'unshackled', that a transformation is in progress. This, of course, is an illusion. Those who know the narcissist, no longer trust his frequent 'conversions', 'decisions', 'crises', 'transformations', 'developments' and 'periods'. They see through his pretensions and declarations into the core of his instability. They know that he is not to be relied upon. They know that with narcissists, temporariness is the only permanence."

We are, therefore, faced with two pathological forms of narcissistic "love".

One type of narcissist "loves" others as one would attach to objects. He "loves" his spouse, for instance, simply because she exists and is available to provide him with Narcissistic Supply. He "loves" his children because they are part of his self-image as a successful husband and father. He "loves" his "friends" because – and only as long as – he can exploit them.

Such a narcissist reacts with alarm and rage to any sign of independence and autonomy in his "charges". He tries to "freeze" everyone around him in their "allocated" positions and "assigned roles". His world is rigid and immovable, predictable and static, fully under his control. He punishes for "transgressions" against this ordained order. He thus stifles life as a dynamic process of compromising and growing – rendering it instead a mere theatre, a tableau vivant.

The other type of narcissist abhors monotony and constancy, equating them, in his mind, with death. He seeks upheaval, drama, and change – but only when they conform to his plans, designs, and views of the world and of himself. Thus, he does not encourage growth in his nearest and dearest. By monopolizing their lives, he, like the other kind of narcissist, also reduces them to mere objects, props in the exciting drama of his life.

This narcissist likewise rages at any sign of rebellion and disagreement. But, as opposed to the first sub-species, he seeks to animate others with his demented energy, grandiose plans, and megalomaniacal self-perception. An adrenaline junkie, his world is a whirlwind of comings and goings, reunions and separations, loves and hates, vocations adopted and discarded, schemes erected and dismantled, enemies turned friends and vice versa. His Universe is equally a theatre, but a more ferocious and chaotic one.

Where is love in all this? Where is the commitment to the loved one's welfare, the discipline, the extension of oneself to incorporate the beloved, the mutual growth?

Nowhere to be seen. The narcissist's "love" is hate and fear disguised – fear of losing control and hatred of the very people his precariously balanced personality so depends on. The narcissist is egotistically committed only to his own well-being. To him, the objects of his "love" are interchangeable and inferior.

He idealizes his nearest and dearest not because he is smitten by emotion – but because he needs to captivate them and to convince himself that they are worthy Sources of Supply, despite their flaws and mediocrity. Once he deems them useless, he discards and devalues them similarly cold-bloodedly. A predator, always on the lookout, he debases the coin of "love" as he corrupts everything else in himself and around him.

Narcissists, Love and Healing

The narcissist hates to be loved because he hates women (is a misogynist); because he fears intimacy (which would render him less unique and less mysterious); and because he cannot believe that an intelligent, perceptive mate would find him loveable.

Question:

Why do narcissists react with rage to gestures or statements of love?

Answer:

Nothing is more hated by the narcissist than the sentence *"I Love You"*. It evokes in him almost primordial reactions. It provokes him to uncontrollable rage. Why is that?

a. The narcissist hates women virulently and vehemently. A misogynist, he identifies being loved with being possessed, encroached upon, shackled, transformed, reduced, exploited, weakened, engulfed, digested and excreted. To him love is a dangerous pursuit, fickle and labile. He believes in fear and hate as immutable, reliable motivations, not in love. He gets married only so as to secure the services of his "partner" as homemaker, audience, personal assistant, and companion. He, therefore, is rarely possessive and jealous: he doesn't care what she does, when, and with whom, as long as his needs and expectations are impeccably met. He avoids intimacy also because it demands reciprocity and, thus, a waste of his scarce and precious resources on the tedious chore of maintaining a relationship when all he wants is a business-like, contractual arrangement.

When a woman tries to pick up a narcissist, flirt with him, or court him, he is likely to react by subjecting her to humiliating and cool disdain (if he is a cerebral narcissist) or by dumping her after having sex with her (somatic narcissist). In both cases the abusive message is: you have no power over me because I am unique, omnipotent, not your typical run-of-the-mill sap; you are nothing to me but a pitiful parasite or an object to be violated. Your very approach and attempt to seduce me is proof of your imbecility, blindness, or maliciousness for how could you not have noticed that I am different and superior?

b. Being loved means being known intimately. The narcissist likes to think that he is so unique and deep that he can never be fathomed. The narcissist believes that he is above mere human understanding and empathy, that he is one of a kind (sui generis). To say to him "I love you", means to negate this feeling, to try to drag him to the lowest common denominator, to threaten his sense of uniqueness. After all, everyone is capable of loving and everyone, even the basest human beings, fall in love. To the narcissist loving is an animalistic and pathological behaviour – exactly like sex.

c. The narcissist knows that he is a con artist, a fraud, an elaborate hoax, a script, hollow and really non-existent. The person who claims to love him is either lying (what is there to love in a narcissist?) – or a self-deceiving, clinging, and immature codependent. The narcissist cannot tolerate the thought that he has chosen a liar or an idiot for a mate. Indirectly, her declaration of love is a devastating critique of the narcissist's own powers of judgement.

The narcissist hates love – however and wherever it is manifested.

Thus, for instance, when his spouse demonstrates her love to their children, he wishes them all ill. He is so pathologically envious of his spouse that he wishes she never existed. Being a tad paranoid, he also nurtures the growing conviction that she is showing love to her children demonstrably and on purpose, to remind him how miserable he is, how deficient, how deprived and discriminated against.

He regards her interaction with their children to be a provocation, an assault on his emotional welfare and balance. Seething envy, boiling rage and violent thoughts form the flammable concoction in the narcissist's mind whenever he sees other people happy.

Many people naively believe that they can cure the narcissist by engulfing him with love, acceptance, compassion and empathy. This is not so. The only time a transformative healing process occurs is when the narcissist experiences a severe narcissistic injury, a life crisis.

Forced to shed his malfunctioning defences, an ephemeral window of vulnerability is formed through which therapeutic intervention can try and sneak in.

The narcissist is susceptible to treatment only when his defences are down because they had failed to secure a steady stream of Narcissistic Supply. The narcissist's therapy aims to wean him off Narcissistic Supply.

But the narcissist perceives other people's love and compassion as forms of Narcissistic Supply!

It is a lose-lose proposition:

If therapy is successful and the narcissist is rid of his addiction to narcissistic supply - he is rendered incapable of giving and receiving love, which he regards as a variety of said supply.

The roles of Narcissistic Supply should be clearly distinguished from those of an emotional bond (such as love), though.

Narcissistic Supply has to do with the functioning of the narcissist's primitive defence mechanisms. The emotional component in the narcissist's psyche is repressed, dysfunctional, and deformed. It is subconscious - the narcissist is not aware of his own emotions and is out of touch with his feelings.

The narcissist pursues Narcissistic Supply as a junkie seeks drugs. Junkies can forms emotional "bonds" but these are always subordinate to their habit. Their emotional interactions are the victims of their habits, as their children and spouses can attest.

It is impossible to have any real, meaningful, or lasting emotional relationship with the narcissist until his primitive defence mechanisms crumble and are discarded. Dysfunctional interpersonal relationships are one of the hallmarks of other personality disorders aswell.

To help the narcissist:

1. Cut him from his Sources of Supply and thus precipitate a narcissistic crisis or injury;

2. Use this window of opportunity and convince the narcissist to attend structured therapy in order to help him mature emotionally;

3. Encourage him in his emotional, self-forming baby steps.

"Emotional" liaisons which co-exist with the narcissist's narcissistic defence mechanisms are part of the narcissistic theatrical repertoire, fake and doomed. The narcissist's defence mechanisms render him a serial monogamist or a non-committal playboy.

The narcissist is unlikely to get rid of his defence mechanisms on his own. He does not employ them because he needs them – but because he knows no different. They proved useful in his infancy. They were adaptive in an abusive environment. Old tricks and old habits die hard.

The narcissist has a disorganised personality [Kernberg]. He may improve and emotionally mature in order to avoid the pain of certain or recurrent narcissistic injuries.

When narcissists do come to therapy, it is to try and alleviate some of what has become an intolerable pain. None of them goes to therapy because he wants to better interact with others. Love is important – but to fully enjoy its emotional benefits, first the narcissist must heal.

Intimacy and Abuse

It is an established fact that abuse – verbal, psychological, emotional, physical, and sexual – co-occurs with intimacy. Most reported offenses are between intimate partners and between parents and children. This defies common sense. Emotionally, it should be easier to batter, molest, assault, or humiliate a total stranger. It's as if intimacy **CAUSES** abuse, incubates and nurtures it.

And, in a way, it does.

Many abusers believe that their abusive conduct fosters, enhances, and cements their intimate relationships. To them, pathological jealousy is proof of love, possessiveness replaces mature bonding, and battering is a form of paying attention to the partner and communicating with her. Psychopaths and narcissists possess "cold empathy": the ability to "see through" people and instantly discern their vulnerabilities, fears, and needs. They leverage this knowledge to foster faux-intimacy with a select few.

This "targeted intimacy" helps to condition the abuser's nearest, dearest, and closest and transform them into a "flock" or an "audience": members of his mini- cult. Targeted intimacy is exclusionary (excludes everyone outside the "cult"); ephemeral (wanes when no longer useful); and utilitarian (intended to manipulate the recipient of the intimacy and its ostensible beneficiary.)

Targeted intimacy is triggered when the abuser sets a goal and embarks on a charm offensive intended to re-acquire a potential source of narcissistic supply or of material benefits by idealizing her. His needs satisfied, the abuser's warm interest in his target abruptly dissipates and he turns cold and distant, devalues and discards. He blames his prey for this startling about-face: she made him withdraw with her nagging, insensitivity, dumbness, insufferable character, hypocrisy, evil designs, and so on.

Such habitual offenders do not know any better. They were often raised in families, societies, and cultures where abuse is condoned outright – or, at least, not frowned upon. Maltreatment of one's significant others is part of daily life, as inevitable as the weather, a force of nature.

Intimacy is often perceived to include a license to abuse. The abuser treats his nearest, dearest, and closest as mere objects, instruments of gratification, utilities, or extensions of himself. He feels that he "owns" his spouse, girlfriend, lovers, children, parents, siblings, or colleagues. As the owner, he has the right to "damage the goods" or even dispose of them altogether.

Most abusers are scared of real intimacy and deep commitment. They lead a "pretend", confabulated life. Their "love" and "relationships" are gaudy, fake imitations. The abuser seeks to put a distance between himself and those who truly love him, who cherish and value him as a human being, who enjoy his company, and who strive to establish a long-term, meaningful relationship with him.

Abuse, in other words, is a reaction to the perceived threat of looming intimacy, aimed at fending it off, intended to decimate closeness, tenderness, affection, and compassion before they thrive and consume the abuser. Abuse is a panic reaction. The batterer, the molester, are scared out of their wits – they feel entrapped, imprisoned, shackled, and insidiously altered.

Lashing out in blind and violent rage they punish the perceived perpetrators of intimacy. The more obnoxiously they behave, the less the risk of lifelong bondage. The more heinous their acts, the safer they feel. Battering, molesting, raping, berating, taunting – are all forms of reasserting lost control. In the abuser's thwarted mind, abuse equals mastery and continued, painless, emotionally numbed, survival.

Dr. Jackal and Mr. Hide: The Cerebral vs. the Somatic Narcissist

Narcissists are either cerebral or somatic. In other words, they either generate their Narcissistic Supply by applying their bodies or by applying their minds.

The somatic narcissist flaunts his sexual conquests, parades his possessions, exhibits his muscles, brags about his physical aesthetics or sexual prowess or exploits, is often a health freak and a hypochondriac. The somatic narcissist regards his body as an object to be sculpted and honed (via extreme diets, multiple cosmetic surgeries, bodybuilding, or weightlifting). When coupled with psychopathic tendencies, the somatic appropriates other people's bodies and treats these as "raw materials" to be dismembered, tampered with, altered, invaded, or otherwise abused.

The cerebral narcissist is a know-it-all, haughty and intelligent "computer". He uses his awesome intellect, or knowledge (real or pretended) to secure adoration, adulation and admiration. To him, his body and its maintenance are a burden and a distraction.

Both types are auto-erotic (psychosexually in love with themselves, with their bodies and with their brain). Both types prefer masturbation to adult, mature, interactive, multi-dimensional and emotion-laden sex.

The cerebral narcissist is often celibate (even when he has a girlfriend or a spouse). He prefers pornography and sexual auto-stimulation to the real thing. The cerebral narcissist is sometimes a latent (hidden, not yet outed) homosexual.

The somatic narcissist uses other people's bodies to masturbate. Sex with him - pyrotechnics and acrobatics aside - is likely to be an impersonal and emotionally alienating and draining experience. The partner is often treated as an object, an extension of the somatic narcissist, a toy, a warm and pulsating vibrator.

It is a mistake to assume type-constancy. In other words, all narcissists are BOTH cerebral and somatic. In each narcissist, one of the types is dominant. So, the narcissist is either OVERWHELMINGLY cerebral - or DOMINANTLY somatic. But the other type, the recessive (manifested less frequently) type, is there. It is lurking, waiting to erupt.

The narcissist swings between his dominant type and his recessive type. The latter is expressed mainly as a result of a major narcissistic injury or life crisis.

Personal example:

I am a cerebral narcissist. I brandish my brainpower, exhibit my intellectual achievements, bask in the attention given to my mind and its products. I hate my body and neglect it. It is a nuisance, a burden, a derided appendix, an inconvenience, a punishment. Needless to add that I rarely have sex (often years apart). I masturbate regularly, very mechanically, as one would change water in an aquarium. I stay away from women because I perceive them to be ruthless predators who are out to consume me and mine.

I have had quite a few major life crises. I got divorced, lost millions a few times, did time in one of the worst prisons in the world, fled countries as a political refugee, was threatened, harassed and stalked by powerful people and groups. I have been devalued, betrayed, denigrated and insulted.

Invariably, following every life crisis, the somatic narcissist in me took over. I became a lascivious lecher. When this happened, I had a few relationships - replete with abundant and addictive sex - going simultaneously. I participated in and initiated group sex and mass orgies. I exercised, lost weight and honed my body into an irresistible proposition.

This outburst of unrestrained, primordial lust waned in a few months and I settled back into my cerebral ways. No sex, no women, no body.

These total reversals of character stun my mates. My girlfriends and spouse found it impossible to digest this eerie transformation from the gregarious, darkly handsome, well-built and sexually insatiable person that swept them off their feet - to the bodiless, bookwormish hermit with not an inkling of interest in either sex or other carnal pleasures.

I miss my somatic half. I wish I could find a balance, but I know it is a doomed quest. This sexual beast of mine will forever be trapped in the intellectual cage that is I, Sam Vaknin, the Brain.

Female Narcissists - Gender and the Narcissist

The psychodynamics of male and female narcissists are the same.

Women narcissists differ only in the choice of sources of narcissistic supply which often conforms to traditional gender roles and in the willingness to attend therapy.

Question:

Are female narcissists any different? You seem to talk only about male narcissists!

Answer:

I keep using the male third person singular because most narcissists (75%) are males and more so because there is little difference between the male and female narcissists.

In the manifestation of their narcissism, female and male narcissists, inevitably, do tend to differ. They emphasise different things. They transform different elements of their personalities and of their lives into the cornerstones of their disorder.

Women concentrate on their body (many also suffer from eating disorders: Anorexia Nervosa and Bulimia Nervosa). They flaunt and exploit their physical charms, their sexuality, their socially and culturally determined "femininity". They secure their Narcissistic Supply through their more traditional gender role: the home, children, suitable careers, their husbands ("the wife of…"), their feminine traits, their role in society, etc.

It is no wonder than narcissists – both men and women – are chauvinistic and conservative. They depend to such an extent on the opinions of people around them – that, with time, they are transformed into ultra-sensitive seismographs of public opinion, barometers of prevailing social fashions, and guardians of conformity. The narcissist cannot afford to seriously alienate his "constituency", those people who reflect his False Self back to him. The very proper and on-going functioning of the narcissist's Ego depends on the goodwill and the collaboration of his human environment.

True, besieged and consumed by pernicious guilt feelings – many a narcissist finally seek to be punished. The self-destructive narcissist then plays the role of the "bad guy" (or "bad girl"). But even then it is within the traditional socially allocated roles. To ensure social opprobrium (read: attention), the narcissist exaggerates these roles to a caricature.

A woman is likely to label herself a "whore" and a male narcissist to self-style himself a "vicious, unrepentant criminal". Yet, these again are traditional social roles. Men are likely to emphasise intellect, power, aggression, money, or social status. Women are likely to emphasise body, looks, charm, sexuality, feminine "traits", homemaking, children and childrearing – even as they seek their masochistic punishment.

Another difference is in the way the genders react to treatment. Women are more likely to resort to therapy because they are more likely to admit to psychological problems. But while men may be less inclined to **DISCLOSE** or to expose their problems to others (the macho-man factor) – it does not necessarily imply that they are less prone to admit it to themselves. Women are also more likely to ask for help than men.

Yet, the prime rule of narcissism must never be forgotten: the narcissist uses everything around him or her to obtain his (or her) Narcissistic Supply. Children happen to be more attached to the female narcissist due to the way our society is still structured and to the fact that women are the ones to give birth. It is easier for a woman to think of her children as her extensions because they once indeed were her physical extensions and because her on-going interaction with them is both more intensive and more extensive.

This means that the male narcissist is more likely to regard his children as a nuisance than as a source of rewarding Narcissist Supply – especially as they grow older and become autonomous. Devoid of the diversity of alternatives available to men – the narcissistic woman fights to maintain her most reliable Source of Supply: her children. Through insidious indoctrination, guilt formation, emotional sanctions, deprivation and other psychological mechanisms, she tries to induce in them a dependence, which cannot be easily unravelled.

But, there is no psychodynamic difference between children, money, or intellect, as Sources of Narcissistic Supply. So, there is no psychodynamic difference between male and female narcissist. The only difference is in their choices of Sources of Narcissistic Supply.

There are mental disorders, which afflict a specific sex more often. This has to do with hormonal or other physiological dispositions, with social and cultural conditioning through the socialisation process, and with role assignment through the gender differentiation process. None of these seem to be strongly correlated to the formation of malignant narcissism. The Narcissistic Personality Disorder (as opposed, for instance, to the Borderline or the Histrionic Personality Disorders, which afflict women more than men) seems to conform to social mores and to the prevailing ethos of capitalism. Social thinkers like Lasch speculated that modern American culture – a narcissistic, self-centred one – increases the rate of incidence of the Narcissistic Personality Disorder. As Kernberg observed:

"The most I would be willing to say is that society can make serious psychological abnormalities, which already exist in some percentage of the population, seem to be at least superficially appropriate."

Quotes from the Literature

"Specifically, past research suggests that exploitive tendencies and open displays of feelings of entitlement will be less integral to narcissism for females than for males. For females such displays may carry a greater possibility of negative social sanctions because they would violate stereotypical gender-role expectancies for women, who are expected to engage in such positive social behavior as being tender, compassionate, warm, sympathetic, sensitive, and understanding.

In females, Exploitiveness/Entitlement is less well-integrated with the other components of narcissism as measured by the Narcissistic Personality Inventory (NPI) - Leadership/Authority, Self-absorption/Self-admiration, and Superiority/Arrogance- than in males - though 'male and female narcissists in general showed striking similarities in the manner in which most of the facets of narcissism were integrated with each other'."

<u>*Gender differences in the structure of narcissism: a multi-sample analysis of the narcissistic personality inventory*</u> *- Brian T. Tschanz, Carolyn C. Morf, Charles W. Turner* **-Sex Roles: A Journal of Research -** *Issue: May, 1998*

"Women leaders are evaluated negatively if they exercise their authority and are perceived as autocratic."

Eagly, A. H., Makhijani, M. G., & Klonsky, B. G. (1992). Gender and the evaluation of leaders: A meta-analysis. Psychological Bulletin, 111, 3-22, and ...

Butler, D., & Gels, F. L. (1990). Nonverbal affect responses to male and female leaders: Implications for leadership evaluations. Journal of Personality and Social Psychology, 58, 48-59.

"Competent women must also appear to be sociable and likable in order to influence men - men must only appear to be competent to achieve the same results with both genders."

Carli, L. L., Lafleur, S. J., & Loeber, C. C. (1995). Nonverbal behavior, gender, and influence. Journal of Personality and Social Psychology, 68, 1030-1041.

Gender Bias in Diagnosing Personality Disorders

Ever since Freud, more women than men sought therapy. Consequently, terms like "hysteria' are intimately connected to female physiology and alleged female psychology. The DSM

(Diagnostic and Statistical Manual, the bible of the psychiatric profession) expressly professes gender bias: personality disorders such as Borderline and Histrionic are supposed to be more common among women. but the DSM is rather even-handed: other personality disorders (e.g., the Narcissistic and Antisocial as well as the Schizotypal, Obsessive-Compulsive, Schizoid, and Paranoid) are more prevalent among men.

Why this gender disparity? There are a few possible answers:

Maybe personality disorders are not objective clinical entities, but culture-bound syndromes. In other words, perhaps they reflect biases and value judgments. Some patriarchal societies are also narcissistic. They emphasize qualities such as individualism and ambition, often identified with virility. Hence the preponderance of pathological narcissism among men. Women, on the other hand, are widely believed to be emotionally labile and clinging. This is why most Borderlines and Dependents are females.

Upbringing and environment, the process of socialization and cultural mores all play an important role in the pathogenesis of personality disorders. These views are not fringe: serious scholars (e.g., Kaplan and Pantony, 1991) claim that the mental health profession is inherently sexist.

Then again, genetics may be is at work. Men and women do differ genetically. This may account for the variability of the occurrence of specific personality disorders in men and women.

Some of the diagnostic criteria are ambiguous or even considered "normal" by the majority of the population. Histrionics "consistently use physical appearance to draw attention to self." Well, who doesn't in Western society? Why when a woman clings to a man it is labeled "codependence", but when a man relies on a woman to maintain his home, take care of his children, choose his attire, and prop his ego it is "companionship" (Walker, 1994)?

The less structured the interview and the more fuzzy the diagnostic criteria, the more the diagnostician relies on stereotypes (Widiger, 1998).

Homosexual and Transsexual Narcissists

Homosexual narcissists are auto-erotic and somatic: they leverage their body and sexuality to obtain narcissistic supply.

Transsxual narcissists feel entitled to special treatment and cosseting.

Question:

What is the typical profile of a homosexual narcissist? Why is he always on a lookout for new victims? Is he lying or is he telling the truth when he says that he "wants to get laid" by one and all? If he is not suicidal, is he not afraid of AIDS?

Answer:

I am a heterosexual and thus deprived of an intimate acquaintance with certain psychological processes, which allegedly are unique to homosexuals. I find it hard to believe that there are such processes, to begin with. Research failed to find any substantive difference between the psychological make-up of a narcissist who happens to have homosexual preferences – and a heterosexual narcissist.

They both are predators, devouring Narcissistic Supply Sources as they go. Narcissists look for new victims, the way tigers look for prey – they are hungry. Hungry for adoration, admiration, acceptance, approval, and any other kind of attention. Old sources die easy – once taken for granted, the narcissistic element of conquest vanishes.

Conquest is important because it proves the superiority of the narcissist. The very act of subduing, subjugating, or acquiring the power to influence someone provides the narcissist with Narcissistic Supply. The newly conquered idolise the narcissist and serve as a trophies.

The act of conquering and subordinating is epitomized by the sexual encounter - an objective and atavistic interaction. Making love to someone means that the consenting partner finds the narcissist (or one or more of his traits, such as his intelligence, his physique, even his money) irresistible.

The distinction between passive and active sexual partners is mechanical, false, superfluous and superficial. Penetration does not make one of the parties "the stronger one". To cause someone to have sex with you is a powerful stimulus – and always provokes a sensation of omnipotence. Whether one is physically passive or active – one is always psychosexually active.

Anyone who has unsafe sex is gambling with his life – though the odds are much smaller than public hysteria would have us believe. Reality does not matter, though – it is the perception of reality that matters. Getting this close to (perceived) danger is the equivalent of engaging in self-destruction (suicide). Narcissists are, at times, suicidal and are always self-destructive.

There is, however, one element, which might be unique to homosexuals: the fact that their self-definition hinges on their sexual identity. I know of no heterosexual who would use his sexual preferences to define himself almost fully. Homosexuality has been inflated to the level of a sub-culture, a separate psychology, or a myth. This is typical of persecuted minorities. However, it does have an influence on the individual. Preoccupation with body and sex makes most homosexual narcissists **SOMATIC** narcissists.

Moreover, the homosexual makes love to a person of the *SAME* sex – in a way, to his **REFLECTION**. In this respect, homosexual relations are highly narcissistic and autoerotic affairs.

The somatic narcissist directs his libido at his body (as opposed to the cerebral narcissist, who concentrates upon his intellect). He cultivates it, nourishes and nurtures it, is often an hypochondriac, dedicates an inordinate amount of time to its needs (real and imaginary). It is through his body that this type of narcissist tracks down and captures his Supply Sources.

The supply that the somatic narcissist so badly requires is derived from his form, his shape, his build, his profile, his beauty, his physical attractiveness, his health, his age. He downplays Narcissistic Supply directed at other traits. He uses sex to reaffirm his prowess, his attractiveness, or his youth. Love, to him, is synonymous with sex and he focuses his learning skills on the sexual act, the foreplay and the coital aftermath.

Seduction becomes addictive because it leads to a quick succession of Supply Sources. Naturally, boredom (a form of transmuted aggression) sets in once the going gets routine. Routine is counter-narcissistic by definition because it threatens the narcissist's sense of uniqueness.

An interesting side issue relates to transsexuals.

Philosophically, there is little difference between a narcissist who seeks to avoid his True Self (and positively to become his False Self) – and a transsexual who seeks to discard his true gender. But this similarity, though superficially appealing, is questionable.

People sometimes seek sex reassignment because of advantages and opportunities which, they believe, are enjoyed by the other sex. This rather unrealistic (fantastic) view of the other is faintly narcissistic. It includes elements of idealised over-valuation, of self-preoccupation, and of objectification of one's self. It demonstrates a deficient ability to empathise and some grandiose sense of entitlement ("I deserve to be taken care of") and omnipotence ("I can be whatever I want to be – despite nature/God").

This feeling of entitlement is especially manifest in some gender dysphoric individuals who aggressively pursue hormonal or surgical treatment. They feel that it is their inalienable right to receive it on demand and without any strictures or restrictions. For instance, they oftentimes refuse to undergo psychological evaluation or treatment as a condition for the hormonal or surgical treatment.

It is interesting to note that both narcissism and gender dysphoria are early childhood phenomena. This could be explained by problematic Primary Objects, dysfunctional families, or a common genetic or biochemical problem. It is too early to say which. As yet, there isn't even an agreed typology of gender identity disorders – let alone an in-depth comprehension of their sources.

A radical view, proffered by Ray Blanchard, seems to indicate that pathological narcissism is more likely to be found among non-core, ego-dystonic, autogynephilic transsexulas and among heterosexual transvestites. It is less manifest in core, ego-syntonic, homosexual transsexuals.

Autogynephilic transsexuals are subject to an intense urge to become the opposite sex and, thus, to be rendered the sexual object of their own desire. In other words, they are so sexually attracted to themselves that they wish to become both lovers in the romantic equation - the male and the female. It is the fulfilment of the ultimate narcissistic fantasy with the False Self as a fetish ("narcissistic fetish").

Autogynephilic transsexuals start off as heterosexuals and end up as either bisexual or homosexual. By shifting his/her attentions to men, the male autogynephilic transsexual "proves" to himself that he has finally become a "true" and desirable woman.

Narcissists and Women

Narcissists are misogynists, women-haters. Women represent sex, intimacy, and family and, therefore, mediocrity.

The narcissist divides all women into sluttish huntresses and sexless saints. He aims to frustrate and subjugate them.

Question:

Do narcissists hate women?

Answer:

Click HERE to Watch the Video

Women are sources of narcissistic supply (which the narcissist craves) and of intimacy (which the narcissist fears).

Narcissists are addicted to a drug called "narcissistic supply". Primary Narcissistic Supply (PNS) is any kind of NS provided by people who are not "meaningful" or "significant" others. Adulation, attention, affirmation, fame, notoriety, sexual conquests are all forms of PNS. Secondary NS (SNS) emanates from people who are in repetitive or continuous touch with the narcissist (such as his female spouse or lover). Secondary Narcissistic Supply includes the important roles of narcissistic accumulation (remembering and witnessing the narcissist's "moments of glory") and narcissistic regulation (reminding the narcissist of these moments when he is running low on narcissistic supply). Narcissists, therefore, need women to carry out these functions. They are dependent on women.

But narcissists also abhor and dread getting emotionally intimate. Sex is perceived as the ultimate act of intimacy. Hence, narcissists try to either avoid sex altogether or transform it into an impersonal act. Cerebral narcissists regard sex as a maintenance chore, something they have to do in order to keep their Source of Secondary Supply content and around. The somatic narcissist treats women as objects and sex as a means to obtaining Narcissistic Supply. Thus, the narcissist's frame of mind is reminiscent of that of the European male well into the 18th century: women and children are perceived as property (chattel), their role is the unconditional and prompt gratification of the narcissist.

Moreover, many narcissists tend to frustrate women. They refrain from having sex with them, tease them and then leave them, resist flirtatious and seductive behaviours and so on. Often, they invoke the existence of a girlfriend/fiancée/spouse as the "reason" why they cannot have sex or develop a relationship. But this is not out of loyalty and fidelity in the empathic and loving sense. This is because they wish (and often succeed) to sadistically frustrate the interested party.

But, this pertains only to cerebral narcissists - not to somatic narcissists and to Histrionics (Histrionic Personality Disorder - HPD) who use their body, sexuality, and seduction/flirtation to extract Narcissistic Supply from others.

Narcissists are misogynists. They team up with women who serve as Sources of SNS (Secondary Narcissistic Supply). The woman's chores are to accumulate past Narcissistic Supply (by witnessing the narcissist's "moments of glory") and release it in an orderly manner to regulate the fluctuating flow of primary supply and compensate in times of deficient supply.

Otherwise, cerebral narcissists are not interested in women.

Most of them are asexual (desire sex very rarely, if at all). They hold women in contempt and abhor the thought of being really intimate with them. Usually, they choose for partners submissive women whom they disdain for being well below their intellectual level.

This leads to a vicious cycle of neediness and self-contempt ("How come I am dependent on this inferior woman"). Hence the abuse. When Primary NS is available, the woman is hardly tolerated, as one would reluctantly pay the premium of an insurance policy.

Narcissists of all stripes do regard the "subjugation" of an attractive woman to be a Source of Narcissistic Supply, though.

Such conquests are status symbols, proofs of virility, and they allow the narcissist to engage in "vicarious" narcissistic behaviours, to express his narcissism through the "conquered" women, transforming them into instruments at the service of his narcissism, into his extensions. This is done by employing defence mechanisms such as projective identification.

The narcissist believes that being in love is actually merely going through the motions. To him, emotions are mimicry and pretence.

He says: "I am a conscious misogynist. I fear and loathe women and tend to ignore them to the best of my ability. To me they are a mixture of hunter and parasite."

Most male narcissists are misogynists. After all, they are the warped creations of women. Women gave birth to them and moulded them into what they are: dysfunctional, maladaptive, and emotionally dead. They are angry at their mothers and, by extension at all women.

The narcissist's attitude to women is, naturally, complex and multi-layered but it can be described using four axes:

1. The Holy Whore
2. The Hunter Parasite
3. The Frustrating Object of Desire
4. Uniqueness Roles

The narcissist divides all women to saints and whores. He finds it difficult to have sex ("dirty", "forbidden", "punishable", "degrading") with feminine significant others (spouse, intimate girlfriend). To him, sex and intimacy are mutually exclusive rather than mutually expressive propositions.

Click HERE to Watch the Video

Sex is reserved to "whores" (all other women in the world). This division resolves the narcissist's constant cognitive dissonance ("I want her but …", "I don't need anyone but …"). It also legitimises his sadistic urges (abstaining from sex is a major and recurrent narcissistic "penalty" inflicted on female "transgressors"). It tallies well with the frequent idealisation-devaluation cycles the narcissist goes through. The idealised females are sexless, the devalued ones – "deserving" of their degradation (sex) and the contempt that, inevitably, follows thereafter.

Sigmund Freud wrote: *"Where they love they do not desire and where they desire they cannot love … The main protective measure … consists in a psychical debasement of the sexual object, the overvaluation … being reserved for the incestuous object (mother-like spouse or girlfriend – SV) … As soon as the condition of debasement is fulfilled, sensuality can be freely expressed and important sexual capacities and a high degree of pleasure can develop."* (S. Freud, "On the Universal Tendency to Debasement in the Sphere of Love", 1912.)

The narcissist believes firmly that women are out to "hunt" men by genetic predisposition. As a result, he feels threatened (as any prey would). This, of course, is an intellectualisation of the real state of affairs: the narcissist feels threatened by women and tries to justify this irrational fear by imbuing them with "objective", menacing qualities. This is a small detail in a larger canvass. The narcissist "pathologises" others in order to control them.

The narcissist believes that, once their prey is secured, women assume the role of "body snatchers". They abscond with the male's sperm, generate an endless stream of demanding and nose dripping children, financially bleed the men in their lives to cater to their needs and to the needs of their dependants.

Put differently, women are parasites, leeches, whose sole function is to suck dry every man they find and tarantula-like decapitate him once no longer useful. This, of course, is exactly what the narcissist does to people. Thus, his view of women is a projection.

Heterosexual narcissists desire women as any other red-blooded male does or even more so due to their special symbolic nature in the narcissist's life. Humbling a woman in acts of faintly sado-masochistic sex is a way of getting back at mother. But the narcissist is frustrated by his inability to meaningfully interact with women, by their apparent emotional depth and powers of psychological penetration (real or attributed) and by their sexuality.

Women's incessant demands for intimacy are perceived by the narcissist as a threat. He recoils instead of getting closer. The cerebral narcissist also despises and derides sex, as we said before. Thus, caught in a seemingly intractable repetition complex, in approach-avoidance cycles, the narcissist becomes furious at the source of his frustration. Some narcissists set out to do some frustrating of their own. They tease (passively or actively), or they pretend to be asexual and, in any case, they turn down, rather cruelly, any feminine attempt to court them and to get closer.

Sadistically, they tremendously enjoy their ability to frustrate the desires, passions and sexual wishes of women. It makes them feel omnipotent and self-righteous. Narcissists regularly frustrate all women sexually – and significant women in their lives both sexually and emotionally.

Somatic narcissists simply use women as objects and then discard them. They masturbate, using women as "flesh and blood aides". The emotional background is identical. While the cerebral narcissist punishes through abstention – the somatic narcissist penalises through excess.

The narcissist's mother kept behaving as though the narcissist was and is not special (to her). The narcissist's whole life is a pathetic and pitiful effort to prove her wrong. The narcissist constantly seeks confirmation from others that he is special – in other words that he is, that he actually exists.

Women threaten this quest. Sex is "bestial" and "common". There is nothing "special or unique" about sex. Women's sexual needs threaten to reduce the narcissist to the lowest common denominator: intimacy, sex and human emotions. Everybody and anybody can feel, copulate and breed. There is nothing in these activities to set the narcissist apart and above others. And yet women seem to be interested only in these pursuits. Thus, the narcissist emotionally believes that women are the continuation of his mother by other means and in different guises.

The narcissist hates women virulently, passionately and uncompromisingly. His hate is primal, irrational, the progeny of mortal fear and sustained abuse. Granted, most narcissists learn how to disguise, even repress these untoward feelings. But their hatred does swing out of control and erupt from time to time.

To live with a narcissist is an arduous and eroding task. Narcissists are infinitely pessimistic, bad-tempered, paranoid and sadistic in an absent-minded and indifferent manner. Their daily routine is a rigmarole of threats, complaints, hurts, eruptions, moodiness and rage.

The narcissist rails against slights true and imagined. He alienates people. He humiliates them because this is his only weapon against his own humiliation wrought by their indifference. Gradually, wherever he is, the narcissist's social circle dwindles and then vanishes. Every narcissist is also a schizoid, to some extent. A schizoid is not a misanthrope. The narcissist does not necessarily hate people – he simply does not need them. He regards social interactions as a nuisance to be minimised.

The narcissist is torn between his need to obtain Narcissistic Supply (from human beings) – and his fervent wish to be left alone. This wish springs from contempt and overwhelming feelings of superiority.

There are fundamental conflicts between dependence, counter-dependence and contempt, neediness and devaluation, seeking and avoiding, turning on the charm to attract adulation and reacting wrathfully to the minutest "provocations". These conflicts lead to rapid cycling between gregariousness and self-imposed ascetic seclusion.

Such an unpredictable but always bilious and festering ambience, typical of the narcissist's "romantic" liaisons is hardly conducive to love or sex. Gradually, both become extinct. Relationships are hollowed out. Imperceptibly, the narcissist switches to asexual co-habitation.

But the vitriolic environment that the narcissist creates is only one hand of the equation. The other hand involves the woman herself.

As we said, heterosexual narcissists are attracted to women, but simultaneously repelled, horrified, bewitched and provoked by them. They seek to frustrate and humiliate them. Psychodynamically, the narcissist probably visits upon them his mother's sins – but such simplistic explanation does the subject great injustice.

Most narcissists are misogynists. Their sexual and emotional lives are perturbed and chaotic. They are unable to love in any true sense of the word – nor are they capable of developing any measure of intimacy. Lacking empathy, they are unable to offer to their partners emotional sustenance.

Do narcissists miss loving, would they have liked to love and are they angry with their parents for crippling them in this respect?

To the narcissist, these questions are incomprehensible. There is no way they can answer them. Narcissists have never loved. They do not know what is it that they are supposedly missing. Observing it from the outside, love seems to them to be a risible pathology.

Narcissists equate love with weakness. They hate being weak and they hate and despise weak people (and, therefore, the sick, the old and the young). They do not tolerate what they consider to be stupidity, disease and dependence – and love seems to consist of all three. These are not sour grapes. They really feel this way.

Narcissists are angry men – but not because they never experienced love and probably never will. They are angry because they are not as powerful, awe inspiring and successful as they wish they were and, to their mind, deserve to be. Because their daydreams refuse so stubbornly to come true. Because they are their worst enemy. And because, in their unmitigated paranoia, they see adversaries plotting everywhere and feel discriminated against and contemptuously ignored.

Many of them (the borderline narcissists) cannot conceive of life in one place with one set of people, doing the same thing, in the same field with one goal within a decades-old game plan. To them, this is the equivalent of death. They are most terrified of boredom and whenever faced with its daunting prospect, they inject drama or even danger into their lives. This way they feel alive.

The narcissist is a lonely wolf. He is a shaky platform, indeed, on which to base a family, or plans for the future.

The Narcissist and the Opposite Sex

Click HERE to Watch the Video

This chapter deals with the male narcissist and with his "relationships" with women.

It would be correct to substitute one gender for another. Female narcissists treat the men in their lives in a manner indistinguishable from the way male narcissists treat "their" women. I believe that this is the case with same sex narcissist partners.

A good point of departure would be jealousy, or rather, its pathological form, envy.

The narcissist becomes anxious when he grows aware of how romantically jealous (possessive) he is. This is a peculiar response. Normally, anxiety is characteristic of other kinds of interactions with the opposite sex where the possibility of rejection exists. Most men, for instance, feel anxious before they ask a woman to have sex with them.

The narcissist, in contrast, has a limited and underdeveloped spectrum of emotional reactions. Anxiety characterizes all his interactions with the opposite sex and any situation in which there is a remote possibility that he be rejected or abandoned.

Anxiety is an adaptive mechanism. It is the internal reaction to conflict. When the narcissist envies his female mate he is experiencing precisely such an unconscious conflict.

Jealousy is (justly) perceived as a form of transformed aggression. To direct it at the narcissist's female partner (who stands in for the primary object, his Mother) is to direct it at a forbidden object. It triggers a strong feeling of imminent punishment - a likely abandonment (physical or emotional).

But this is merely the "surface" conflict. There is yet another layer, much harder to reach and to decipher.

To feed his envy, the narcissist exercises his imagination. He imagines situations, which justify his negative emotions. If his mate is sexually promiscuous this justifies romantic jealousy – he unconsciously "thinks".

The narcissist is a con artist. He easily substitutes fiction for truth. What commences as an elaborate daydream ends up in the narcissist's mind as a plausible scenario. But, then, if his suspicions are true (they are bound to be - otherwise, why is he jealous?), there is no way he can accept his partner back, says the narcissist to himself. If she is unfaithful - how could the relationship continue?

Infidelity and lack of exclusivity violate the first and last commandment of narcissism: uniqueness.

The narcissist tends to regard his partner's cheating in absolute terms. The "other" guy must be better and more special than he is. Since the narcissist is nothing but a reflection, a glint in the eyes of others, when cast aside by his spouse or mate, he feels annulled and wrecked.

His partner, in this single (real or imagined) act of adultery, is perceived by the narcissist to have passed judgment upon him as a whole - not merely upon this or that aspect of his personality and not merely in connection with the issue of sexual or emotional compatibility.

This perceived negation of his uniqueness makes it impossible for the narcissist to survive in a relationship tainted by jealousy. Yet, there is nothing more dreadful to a narcissist than the ending of a relationship, or abandonment.

Many narcissists strike an unhealthy balance. Being emotionally (and physically or sexually) absent, they drive the partner to find emotional and physical gratification outside the bond. This achieved, they feel vindicated - they are proven right in being jealous.

The narcissist is then able to accept the partner back and to forgive her. After all – he argues - her two-timing was precipitated by the narcissist's own absence and was always under his control. The narcissist experiences a kind of sadistic satisfaction that he possesses such power over his partner.

In provoking the partner to adopt a socially aberrant behavior he sees proof of his mastery. He reads into the subsequent scene of forgiveness and reconciliation the same meaning. It proves both his magnanimity and how addicted to him his partner has become.

The more severe the extramarital affair, the more it provides the narcissist with the means to control his partner through her guilt. His ability to manipulate his partner increases the more forgiving and magnanimous he is. He never forgets to mention to her (or, at least, to himself) how wonderful he is for having thus sacrificed himself.

Here he is - with his unique, superior traits - willing to accept back a disloyal, inconsiderate, disinterested, self centred, sadistic (and, entre nous, most ordinary) partner back. True, henceforth he is likely to invest less in the relationship, to become non-committal, and, probably, to be full of rage and hatred. Still, she is the narcissist's one and only. The more voluptuous, tumultuous, inane the relationship, the better it suits the narcissist's self image.

After all, aren't such tortuous relationships the stuff Oscar winning movies are made of? Shouldn't the narcissist's life be special in this sense, too? Aren't the biographies of great men adorned with such abysses of emotions?

If an emotional or sexual infidelity does occur (and very often it does), it is usually a cry for help by the narcissist's mate. A forlorn cause: this rigidly deformed personality structure is incapable of change.

Usually, the partner is the dependent or avoidant type and is equally inherently incapable of changing anything in her life. Such couples have no common narrative or agenda and only their psychopathologies are compatible. They hold each other hostage and vie for the ransom.

The dependent partner can determine for the narcissist what is right and virtuous and what is wrong and evil as well as enhance and maintain his feeling of uniqueness (by wanting him). She, therefore, possesses the power to manipulate him. Sometimes she does so because years of emotional deprivation and humiliation by the narcissist have made her hate him.

The narcissist - forever "rational", forever afraid to get in touch with his emotions – often divides his relationships with humans to "contractual" and "non contractual", multiplying the former at the expense of the latter. By doing so he drowns the immediate, identifiable, emotional problems (with his partner) in a torrent of irrelevant frivolities (his obligation within numerous other "contractual" "relationships").

The narcissist likes to believe that he is the maker of the decision which type of relationship he establishes with whom. He doesn't even bother to be explicit about it. Sometimes people believe that they have a "contractual" (binding and long-term) relationship with the narcissist, while he entertains an entirely different notion without informing them. These, naturally, are grounds for innumerable disappointments and misunderstandings.

The narcissist often says that he has a contract with his girlfriend/spouse. This contract has emotional articles and administrative-economic articles.

One of the substantive clauses of this contract is emotional and sexual exclusivity.

But the narcissist feels that the fulfillment of his contracts - especially with his female partner - is asymmetrical. He is firmly convinced that he gives and contributes to his relationships more than he receives from them. The narcissist needs to feel deprived and punished, thus upholding the guilty verdict rendered by the primary and all important object in his life (usually, his mother).

The narcissist, though highly amoral (and at times, immoral), holds himself, morally, in high regard. He describes contracts as "sacred" and feels averse to canceling or violating them even if they had expired or are invalidated by the behavior of the other parties.

But the narcissist is not constant and predictable in his judgments. Thus, a violation of the contract by his romantic partner is deemed to be either trivial or nothing less than earth-shattering. If a contract is violated by the narcissist he is invariably tormented by his conscience to the extent of calling the contract (the relationship) off even if the partner judges the violation to be trivial or explicitly forgives the narcissist.

In other words, sometimes the narcissist feels compelled to cancel a contract just because he violated it and in order not to be tormented by his conscience (by his Superego, the internalized voices of his parents and other meaningful adults in his childhood).

But things get even more complex.

The narcissist acts asymmetrically as long as he feels bound by the contract. He tends to judge himself more severely than he judges the other parties to the contract. He forces himself to comply more strenuously than his partners do with the terms of the contract.

But this is because he needs the contract - the relationship - more than the others do.

The annulment or the termination of a contract represent rejection and abandonment, which the narcissist fears most. The narcissist would rather pretend that a contract is still valid than admit to the demise of a relationship. He never violates contracts because he is afraid of the reprisals and of the emotional consequences. But this is not to be confused with developed morals. When confronted with better alternatives - which more efficiently cater to his needs - the narcissist annuls or violates his contracts without thinking twice.

Moreover, not all contracts were created equal in the narcissistic twilight zone. It is the narcissist who retains the power to decide which contracts are to be scrupulously observed and which offhandedly ignored. The narcissist determines which laws (social contracts) to obey and which to break.

He expects society, his partners, his colleagues, his spouse, his children, his parents, his students, his teachers – in short: absolutely everyone – to abide by his rulebook. White collar narcissist criminals, for instance, see nothing wrong with their misconduct. They regard themselves as law-abiding, God-fearing, community-members. Their acts are committed in a mental enclave, a psychological no man's land, where no laws or contracts are binding.

The narcissist is sometimes perceived as whimsical, traitorous, posing and double crossing. The truth is that he is predictable and consistent. He follows one over-riding principle: the principle of Narcissistic Supply.

The narcissist had internalized a bad object. He feels corrupt, deserving to fail, to be disgraced and punished. He is forever surprised and thankful when good things happen to him. Out of touch with his own emotions and with his capabilities, he either exaggerates them or underestimates them.

He is likely to be grateful to his partner - and berate her! - for having chosen him to be her mate. Deep inside, he thinks that no one else would have been (or will be) as foolish, blind, or ignorant to have made this choice. The purported stupidity and blindness of his mate or spouse is substantiated by the very fact that she *is* his mate or spouse. Only a stupid and blind person would have preferred the narcissist, with his myriad deficiencies, to others.

This feeling of a "lucky break" is the true source of the asymmetry in the narcissist's relationships. The partner, having made this incredible choice to live with the narcissist (to bear this cross) is worthy of special consideration in compensation. The narcissist's willing partner - a rarity - warrants special treatment and a special (double) standard. The partner can be unfaithful, withholding (emotionally, financially), be dependent, be abusive, critical and so on - and, yet, be forgiven unconditionally.

This, no doubt, is the direct result of the narcissist's very flawed sense of self worth and of an overpowering sense of inferiority.

This asymmetry is also an effective barrier against the expression of anger, even legitimate anger.

Instead, the narcissist accumulates his grievances every time that the partner takes advantage of the asymmetry (or is perceived by the narcissist to be doing so). The narcissist tries to convince himself that such abuse is an expected result of the daily friction of cohabitation, especially by partners with radically different personalities.

Some of the anger is passively-aggressively expressed. The frequency of sexual relations is reduced. Less sex, less talk, less touch. Sometimes the pent-up aggression erupts explosively in the form of rage attacks. These are usually followed by panicky reactions intended to restore the balance and to reassure the narcissist that he is not about to be abandoned.

Following such rage attacks, the narcissist regresses to passiveness, maudlin tenderness, appeasing gestures, or to wimpish, saccharine, and infantile behavior. The narcissist does not expect or accept same behavior from his partner. She is allowed to be cantankerous to her heart's content without as much as apologizing.

Another hurdle on the narcissist's way to establishing lasting (if not healthy) relationships is his excess rationality and, chiefly, his tendency to generalize on the basis of tenuous and flimsy evidence (hyper-inductiveness).

The narcissist regards abandonment or rejection by his emotional-sexual partners as a final verdict concerning his very ability to have such relationships in the future. Because of the mechanisms of self-denigration I have described, the narcissist is likely to idealize his mate and believe that she must have been uniquely predisposed and "equipped" to cope with him.

He "remembers" the way his partner sacrificed herself on the altar of the relationship. The more convinced the narcissist is that his partner invested extraordinarily in the relationship and the more assured he is that she was uniquely equipped to succeed in it - the more frightened he becomes.

Why the fear?

Because if this partner, as qualified as she was, as desirous of him as she was, failed to sustain the relationship - surely, no one else is likely to succeed. The narcissist believes that he is doomed to an existence of loneliness and destitution. He stands no chance of ever having a resilient, healthy relationship with another partner.

The narcissist would do anything to avoid this conclusion. He begs his partner to return and re-establish the relationship, no matter what transpired. Her very return proves to him that he is worthy, the preferred alternative, someone with whom maintaining a relationship is possible.

The partner, in other words, is the narcissist's equivalent of market research. That he was chosen by the partner is tantamount to receiving a quality award.

This dyad comprised of a "quality inspector" and a "chosen product" is only one of the pairs of roles adopted by the narcissist and his partner. Others include: "the sick" and "the healthy", "the doctor/psychologist" and "the patient", "the poor, underprivileged girl" and "the white knight in shining armor" dyads.

Both roles - the narcissist's and the one willingly (or unwillingly) adopted by the partner - are facets of the narcissist's personality. Through complex projective identification processes and other projective defence mechanisms the narcissist fosters a dialogue between parts of his self, using his partner as a mirror and a communication conduit.

Thus, by fostering such dialogs, the narcissist's relationships have a highly therapeutic value on the one hand. On the other hand they suffer from all the problems of a regime of psychotherapy: transference, counter-transference and the like.

Let us briefly study the pair of roles "sick-healthy" or "patient-doctor". The narcissist can assume either role in this pair.

If the narcissist is the "healthy" one, he attributes to his "sick" partner his own inability to form long-standing, emotion-infused couple relationships. This would be because she is "sick" (sexually hyperactive, "Nymphomaniac", frigid, unable to commit, to be intimate, unjust, moody, or traumatized by events in her past).

The narcissist, on the other hand, judges himself to be homely and striving to establish a "healthy" couple. He interprets the behavior of his partner to support this "theory". His partner displays emergent behaviors, which conform with her role. Sometimes, the narcissist invests less in such a relationship because he regards his mere existence - sane, strong, omnipotent, and omniscient - to be a sufficient investment (a gift, really), voiding the need to add "maintenance efforts" to it.

In the other, converse case, the narcissist labels many of his behavior patterns as "sick". This usually coincides with latent or open hypochondriasis. The partner's health is idealized to form the background with which the narcissist's purported sickness is contrasted. This is a responsibility shifting mechanism. If the narcissist's pathology is deep seated and irreversible - then he cannot be held responsible for his actions, past and future.

This role playing is the narcissist's ways of coping with an insoluble dilemma.

The narcissist is mortally terrified of being abandoned by his partner. This fear drives him to minimize his interactions with his partner to avoid the inevitable pain of rejection. This, in turn, leads exactly to the feared abandonment. The narcissist knows that his behavior instigates that which he is so afraid of.

In a way he is happy about it, because it gives him the illusion that he is in exclusive control of the relationship and of his own fate. His alleged "sickness" helps to explain his unusual conduct.

Ultimately, the narcissist loses his partners in all his relationships. He hates himself for it and is enraged. It is because of the life-threatening magnitude of these negative emotions that they are repressed. Every conceivable psychological defence mechanism is employed to sublimate, transform (through cognitive dissonance), dissociate or re-direct this self-mutilating wrath.

This constant inner turmoil generates unremitting fear manifested in the form of anxiety attacks, or an Anxiety Disorder. In the course of such life crises, the narcissist briefly believes that he is intrinsically deformed and defective and that he is irreparably dysfunctional when it comes to establishing and to maintaining relationships (which is true!).

The narcissist - especially during a life crisis - loses touch with reality. Defective reality tests and even psychotic micro-episodes are common. Narcissists interpret the (fairly common) mismatch between personalities that doomed the relationships in an apocalyptic manner. Dependence, a symbiotic interaction, raises doubts regarding the narcissist's very ability to form relationships.

But throughout all this, the narcissist needs a collaborative partner. He needs someone to serve as a sounding board, a mirror, and a victim. In other words, he needs a Polyandricwoman.

The narcissist thinks of all women as either Monoandric or Polyandric.

The Monoandric woman is psychologically mature. She is usually older and sexually sated. She prefers intimacy and companionship to sexual satisfaction. She is in possession of a mental blueprint, which dictates her short-term goals. In her relationships, she emphasizes compatibility and is predominantly verbal.

The narcissist reacts with fear and repulsion (mixed with rage and the wish to frustrate) to the Monoandric woman. Consciously, though, he realizes that intimacy can be created only with this kind of woman.

The Polyandric woman is young (if not of age, then at heart). She is still sexually curious and varies her sexual partners. She is not adept at creating intimacy and emotional rapport. Because she is more interested in the accumulation of experiences - her life is not guided by a "master plan", or even by medium-term goals.

The narcissist is aware of the transience of his relationship with the Polyandric woman. So, he is attracted to her while being devoured by his fear of abandonment.

The narcissist, almost always, finds himself paired with Polyandric women. They pose no threat of getting emotionally close to him (of being intimate). The incompatibility between the narcissist and Polyandric women is so high and the probability of abandonment and rejection so great - that intimacy is all but excluded.

Moreover, this consuming fear of being left behind leads to a re-enactment of the primordial Oedipal conflict and to a whole set of transference relations with the Polyandricwoman. This inevitably results in the very abandonment the narcissist so dreads. Serious psychological crises follow such relationships (narcissistic trauma or injury).

The narcissist knows (or, if less self-aware, feels) all this. He is not as much attracted to the Polyandric woman as he is repelled by the Monoandric variety. Monoandric women threaten him with two things deemed by the narcissist to be even worse than abandonment: intimacy and a loss of uniqueness. Monoandric women are the venue through which the narcissist can communicate with his very threatening inner world. Last but not least, they want him to settle into a molded non-unique way of life common to virtually all humanity: marriage, children, a career.

On the one hand, there is nothing like children to make the narcissist feel threatened. They are the embodiment of commonness, a reminder of his own, dark, childhood, and an infringement upon his privileges. They compete with him for scarce Narcissistic Supply.

On the other hand, there is nothing like children to boost an habitually flagging ego. In short, nothing like children to create conflict in the tormented soul of the narcissist.

The narcissist does not react to people (or interact with them) as individuals. Rather, he generalizes and tends to treat people as symbols or "classes". This is also true in his relationships with "his" women. Women resent this kind of treatment and, gradually, the narcissist finds it more and more difficult to be himself with them.

Women analyze his body language, his verbal and non-verbal communication and compare their own pathologies to his. They study his behavior patterns and his interactions with his (human) milieu and (non-human) environment. They test their sexual compatibility by having sex with him.

They examine other types of compatibility by cohabiting or by prolonged dating. Their mating decision is based on the data they thus glean plus some "evolutionary survival parameters": the narcissist's genotype (genetic and chemical makeup), his phenotype (his looks and constitution), as well as his access to economic resources.

This is a standard mating procedure with standard mating checklists. The narcissist usually passes the genotype and phenotype reviews. Many narcissists, however, fail the third test: their ability to support themselves and their dependants economically. Narcissism is a very unstable mental condition and it complicates the narcissist's functioning in daily life.

Most narcissists tend to move between numerous positions and jobs, to gamble away their savings, and to become heavily indebted. The narcissist rarely accumulates wealth, property, assets, or possessions. The narcissist prefers to fake knowledge rather than to acquire it and to compromise rather to fight.

He usually finds himself engaged in capacities far below his intellectual ability. Women notice this as well as his pompous, inflated body language, haughtiness, rage attacks and severe acting out. Finally, the closer they get to the narcissist, the more they are be able to discern antisocial, abnormal, and a-normative behaviors.

The narcissist turns out to be a crook, an adventurer, a crisis-prone, danger seeking, emotionally cold, sexually abstaining or hyperactive individual. He might be self-destructive, self-defeating, success-fearing, and media-addicted. His turbulent biography is likely to include abnormal sexual and emotional relationships, prison terms, bankruptcies and divorces. Hardly the ideal partner.

Even worse, the narcissist is likely to be a misogynist. He regards women as a direct threat to his uniqueness, and a potential for degradation. To him, they are the conformity agents of society, the domesticating whips. By forcing him into homemaking, child rearing and the assumption of long term consumer credits (and mortgages), women are likely to reduce the narcissist to a Common Man, an anathema. Women represent an invasion of the narcissist's privacy, unmasking his defence mechanisms by "X-raying" his soul (the narcissist attributes paranormal powers of penetration to women).

They possess the ability to hurt him through abandonment and rejection. The narcissist feels that women are very "business-like, use and discard" type of people. They exploit their capacities for deep psychological insight to further their goals. In other words, they are sinister and are not to be trusted. Their motives should always be questioned.

This is the old fear of intimacy disguised. These are the old phobias: of being controlled, of being assimilated, of losing control, of being hurt, of being vulnerable. This is the deep-rooted feeling of emotional inadequacy. The narcissist believes that, upon closer scrutiny, he will be found lacking emotionally and, thus, unlovable.

It is part of the narcissist's "Con-Artist Effect". The narcissist feels an objective and thorough scrutiny is bound to expose him for what he is: a fake, an impostor, a con man. The narcissist is the chameleon-like "Zelig" - everything to everyone, no one to himself.

Narcissists interact with women emotionally (and later, sexually), or only physically.

When the interaction is emotional, the narcissist feels that he is risking the loss of his uniqueness, that his privacy is invaded, that his defence mechanisms are being unraveled, and that information divulged by him (following the collapse of his defenses) might be abused through destructive criticism or extortion.

The narcissist constantly feels that he is rejected. Even if such rejection is the normal outcome of incompatibility, without any comparative judgment and "rating" – the feeling persists. The narcissist just "knows" that she is not sexually or emotionally exclusive (others preceded him and others will succeed him).

During the initial phases of emotional involvement the narcissist is likely to be told that there was no one like him in the partner's life before. He judges this to be a false and hypocritical statement simply because it is likely to have been uttered before, to others. This prevailing sense of falsity permeates the relationship from the very start.

In the back of his mind the narcissist always remembers that he is "different" (sick). He recognizes that this deformity is likely to thwart any relationship and to lead toabandonment, or at lease to rejection. The seeds of abandonment are embedded in every nascent interaction with a woman. The narcissist has to cope with his special predicament as well as with social changes and the disintegration of the social fabric, which anyhow make sustaining relationship an ever more difficult achievement in today's world.

The alternative, mere corporeal contact, the narcissist finds repellant. There, uniqueness and exclusivity – what the narcissist relishes most - are definitely absent.

This is especially true if an emotional dimension does exist in the relationship. Whereas the narcissist can always convince himself that both his emotions and their background are unique and unprecedented - he is hard pressed to do so concerning the sexual aspect of the relationship. Surely, he hasn't been his lover's first sexual partner and sex is a common and vulgar pursuit.

Still, some narcissists prefer less complicated and less threatening sex: devoid of all emotion, anonymous (group sex, prostitution) or autoerotic (homosexual or masturbation). The sexual partner, in these conditions, lacks identity, is objectified and dehumanized. Exclusivity cannot be demanded of objects and the potential risk of unfaithfulness is happily allayed.

An example that I always use: a narcissist, eating in a restaurant, would rarely feel that his uniqueness is threatened by the fact that thousands of people ate there before him and are likely to do so after his departure. Eating in a restaurant is an impersonal, objectified, routine.

The notion of his own uniqueness is so fragile that the narcissist requires "total compliance" in order to be able to maintain it.

Thus, the emotional and sexual exclusivity of his partner (a pillar in the temple of his uniqueness) must be both spatial and temporal. To satisfy the narcissist, the partner must be sexually and emotionally exclusive in both her past and her present. This sounds highly possessive - and it is. The narcissist shivers at the thought of his partner's past lovers and her exploits with them. He is even jealous of movie actors, whom his partner finds appealing.

This need not deteriorate into active, violent jealousy. In most cases, it is an insidious form of envy, which poisons the relationship through mutated forms of aggression.

The narcissist's possessiveness is geared to safeguard his self-imputed uniqueness. The partner's exclusivity enhances the narcissist's sensation of uniqueness. But why can't the narcissist be unique to his partner today as others have been to her in the past?

Because serial uniqueness is a contradiction in terms, uniqueness means ultimate compatibility, enzyme and substrate, protein and receptor, antigen and antibody, almost immunological specificity. The likelihood of serially enjoying precisely such compatibility with successive partners is very low.

For serial compatibility to occur the following conditions have to be met (believes the narcissist):

a. That one (or both) of the partners will have changed so radically that the former specifications of compatibility are replaced by new ones. This radical change can come from the inside (endogenous) or from the outside (exogenous). Such a dramatic shift must, therefore, occur with every new partner.
b. Or that each partner is even more specifically compatible than its predecessor – a highly unlikely occurrence.
c. Or that compatibility is never achieved and one (or both) partners react badly to some of the specifications and initiates separation in order to move on to a more suitable partner
d. Or that compatibility is never achieved and any claim to the contrary (especially the sentence "I love you") is false. The relationship, in this case, is contaminated by major hypocrisy.

Yet, narcissists do get married. They do try to have lifetime partners. This is because they distinguish "their" women from all other. The narcissist's occasional girlfriend (however "permanent") and his permanent partner (however randomly chosen) must satisfy different requirements .

The permanent partner (wife, usually) must meet four conditions:

She must act as the narcissist's companion but on highly unequal terms. She must be submissive and motherly, sufficiently intelligent to admire and admiring enough never to criticize, critical enough to assist him and helpful enough to make a good friend. This contradictory equation can never be solved and leads to bouts of frustration and rage staged by the narcissist if any of his demands or expectations goes unheeded.

The narcissist's partner has to share quarters with him. But the narcissist, with an inflated sense of privacy and what can be best described as spatial paranoia, is very hard to live with. He regards her presence in his space as intrusion. The fragile or non-existent boundaries of his ego force him to define rigid outer boundaries for fear of being "invaded".

He enforces his brand of compulsive orderliness and his code of conduct on his entire physical space in the most tyrannical manner.

It is a hybrid, almost transcendental existence led by the narcissist's mate or spouse. There when required by him, making herself absent at all other times. Rarely can she define her own space or impress her personal preferences and tastes upon it.

The cerebral narcissist's partner is usually his only sexual mate. Cerebral narcissists are normally very faithful because they are mortally afraid of the repercussions if found out cheating. But, being purely Sexual Communicators, they get bored very easily and find it ever more taxing to maintain regular (let alone exciting) sexual relations with the same partner.

They are under-stimulated and for want of alternatives, they develop a vicious frustration-aggression cycle, leading to emotional absence and coldness and to sexual intercourse decreasing in both quality and quantity. This could drive the partner to having extramarital sexual (or, even emotional) affairs.

It provides the narcissist with the justification that he needs to do the same. However, the narcissist rarely uses this license. Instead he leverages the partner's inevitable guilt feelings to deepen his control over her and to place himself in a morally superior position.

Often, the narcissist destabilizes the relationship and keeps his partner off-balance, in constant uncertainty and insecurity by suggesting an open marriage, possible participation in group sex and so on. Or, he constantly alludes to sexual opportunities available to him. This he might do jokingly but he ignores his partner's avid protestations. By provoking her jealousy, the narcissist believes that he endears himself to her and furthers his control.

Last - but definitely not least - is the issue of procreation and of having offspring.

Narcissists like children only as unlimited sources of Narcissistic Supply. Put simply: children unconditionally admire the father-narcissist, they succumb to his every wish, submit to his every whim, obey his every command, and are deliciously malleable.

All other aspects of child-rearing are considered by the narcissist to be repulsive: the noises, the smells, the invasion of his space, the nuisance, the dangers, the long term commitment and, above all, the diversion of attention and admiration from the narcissist to his offspring. The narcissist envies his successful offspring as he would any other competitor for adulation and attention.

A profile of the narcissist's spouse emerges:

She must value the narcissist's companionship sufficiently to sacrifice any independent expression of her personality. She must usually endure confinement in her own home. She either refrains from bringing children to the world altogether or sacrifices them to the narcissist as instruments of his gratification. She must endure long spells of sexual abstinence or be sexually molested by the narcissist.

This is a vicious cycle. The narcissist is likely to devalue such a submissive partner. The narcissist detests self-sacrifice and self-effacement. He scorns such behavior in others. He humiliates his partner until she leaves him and, thus, proves that she is assertive and autonomous. Then, of course, he idealizes her and wants her back.

The narcissist is interested in the kind of woman that he is able to drive to abandon him by sadistically berating and humiliating her (on what could be regarded as justified grounds).

In his internal dialogues, the narcissist mulls over his problematic experience with the opposite sex.

A far as he is concerned, women are emotional objects, instant narcissistic solutions. As long as they are indiscriminately supportive, adoring and admiring they fulfill the critical role of source of narcissistic supply.

We are on safe ground, therefore, when we say that mentally stable and healthy women refrain from having relationships with narcissists.

The narcissist's lifestyle, his reactions, in short: his disorder, prevent the development of a mature love, of real sharing, of empathy. The narcissist's mate, spouse, or partner is treated as an object. She is the subject of projections, projective identifications and a source of adulation.

Moreover, the narcissist himself is unlikely to cultivate a long-term relationship with a psychologically healthy, independent, and mature woman. He seeks her dependence within a relationship of superiority and inferiority (teacher-student, guru-disciple, idol-admirer, therapist-patient, doctor-patient, father-daughter, adult-adolescent or young girl, etc.).

The narcissist is an anachronism. He is a Victorian arch conservative, even if he denies it vehemently. He rejects feminism. He feels ill at ease in today's modern world and is seldom self-conscious enough to understand why. He pretends to be a liberal. But this conviction does not sit well with his envy, an integral element of his narcissistic personality.

His conservatism and jealousy combine to yield extreme possessiveness and a powerful fear of abandonment. The latter can (and does) bring about <u>self-defeating and self-destructive behaviors</u>. These, in turn, encourage the partner to abandon the narcissist. The narcissist, thus, feels that he has aided and abetted the process, that he facilitated his own abandonment.

This is all part of a facade whose genesis can only be partially attributed to repression or denial mechanisms. This fake front is coherent, consistent, ubiquitous and completely misleading. The narcissist uses it to project both his cognition (the results of conscious thought processes) and his affect (emotions).

The narcissist, for instance, would adopt the role of a warm, sensitive, considerate and empathic person - while, in truth, he is likely to be emotionally shallow, to have attention deficits, to be inordinately self centred, insensitive and unaware of what is happening around him and to other people.

He makes promises casually, plagiarizes with abandon, and pathologically (compulsively and unnecessarily) lies - all part of the same phenomenon: a promising, impressive front behind, which are concealed psychical "Potemkin Villages". This makes him the target of strong frustration, hate, hostility and even verbal, physical or legal violence.

The same scenario applies to matters of the heart. The narcissist employs the same tactics with women.

The narcissist lies because he thinks his reality is too "grey" and unattractive. He feels that his skills, traits, and experience are lacking, that his biography is boring, that many aspects of his life call for improvement. The narcissist desperately wants to be loved - and modifies and mends himself to render himself loveable.

To this there is only one exception.

The Sociologist Erving Goffman coined the phrase "Total Institutions". He was referring to institutions with total regulation of the totality of life within them. The army is such an institution and so is a hospital, or a prison. To some extent, any alien environment is total. Living outside one's country, in a foreign, somewhat xenophobic and hostile, society, is reminiscent of living in a Total Institution ("Total Situation").

The mental health problems of some narcissists grow worse in such institutions - and this is understandable. There is nothing like a total institution to negate uniqueness.

But others feel relaxed and secure. How come?

This is an enigma the solution to which provides us with important insights regarding the codes, which control the narcissist's attitudes towards women.

Total Institutions and Total Situations have a few common denominators:

  a. They eliminate the individual's idiosyncratic identity through external measures such as donning uniforms, sleeping in dormitories, using numbers instead of names. In hospitals the patients are identified by their organs or conditions, for instance. But this is counterweighed by a sense of emerging, compensatory uniqueness, the result of belonging to a mysterious select few, an order of suffering or guilt, a brotherhood of endurance.
  b. People in these places have no past or future. They live in an infinite present.
  c. The starting conditions of all the inmates are identical. There are no relative or absolute advantages, no value judgments, no rating of worthiness, no competition, no inferiority or superiority complexes induced from the outside. This, naturally, is a gross oversimplification, even, to some extent, a misstatement of the facts - but we need to idealize in order to analyze.
  d. The Total Institution offers no frame of reference or of comparison which might foster feelings of failure or of inferiority.
  e. The constant threat of sanctions restrains and constrains destructive behaviors. A heightened awareness of reality is necessary for survival. Any self-injury or sabotage is punished more severely than in the outside, "relative", world.

Thus, the narcissist can attribute any failure to his new environment.

If his new environment is the outcome of a voluntary choice (for instance, emigration) the narcissist can say that it was he who chose failure over success - a choice that indeed he made.

Otherwise, the failure is ascribed to overriding external imperatives ("force majeure"). The narcissist has an alternative in this case. He doesn't have to identify with his failures or to internalize them because he can convincingly argue (mainly to himself) that they are not his, that success was impossible under the objective circumstances.

Coping with recurrent failure is a figment of the narcissist's inner life. The narcissist would tend to regard himself as a failure. He doesn't say: "I failed" - but "I am a failure". Whenever he fails - and he is predisposed to fail - he "assimilates" the failure and identifies with it in an act of transubstantiation.

Narcissists are more prone to failure because of their built-in precariousness, instability and their tendency for brinkmanship. The schism between their rational apparatus and their emotional one doesn't help, either. While, usually, highly talented and intelligent - narcissists are emotionally immature and pathological.

Narcissists know that they are inferior to other people in that they are self-defeating and self-destructive. They solve this gap between their grandiose fantasies and their sordid and drab reality (the Grandiosity Gap) by manufacturing and designing their own failures. This way they feel that they control their misfortune.

Obviously, this apparently ingenious mechanism is, in itself, destructive.

On the one hand, it succeeds to make the narcissist feel that he is in control of his failures (if not of his life). On the other hand, the fact that the failure directly and unequivocally emanates from the narcissist - makes it an inseparable part of him. Thus, the narcissist feels not only that he is the author of his own failures (which, in some cases, he, indeed, is) - but that failure forms an integral part of himself (which, gradually, becomes true).

It is due to this identification with his failures, defeats and mishaps, that the narcissist finds it hard to "market" himself, be it to a potential employer or to a woman he desires. T

The narcissist holds himself to be a total (systemic) failure. His self-esteem and self-image are always crippled. He feels that he doesn't have "anything to offer". When he tries to derive consolation from the memory of past successes - the comparison depresses him even further, making him feel that he is in at a nadir.

As it is, the narcissist regards any need to promote himself as demeaning. One promotes oneself because one needs others, because one is inferior (however temporarily). This reliance on others is both external (economic, for example) and internal (emotional). The narcissist is also afraid of the possibility of being rejected, of failing at his self-promotion. This kind of failure may have the worst effect, compounding the narcissist's feeling of worthlessness.

No wonder that the narcissist regards any necessity to self-promote as humiliating, as negating his self-respect in a cold, alienated, transactional universe. The narcissist fails to understand why he needs to promote himself when his uniqueness is so self-evident. He envies the successes and the happiness of others (their successful self-promotion).

None of these problems arises in a Total Institution or outside the narcissist's natural milieu (abroad, for instance), or in a Total Situation.

In these settings, failure can be explained away by being attributed to poor starting conditions inherent in a new envirnment. The narcissist does not have to internalize the failure or to identify with it. The act of self-promotion is also made much easier. It is understandable why one has to promote oneself if one is rendered inferior or unknown by circumstances of one's choice.

In total situations, the need to market oneself is understandable, external, and objective, a force majeure, really, though brought about by the narcissist himself. The narcissist compares the situation to a game of chess: you select which game to play but once you have done so, you have to abide by the rules, however disadvantageous.

In these circumstances failure can be attributed to outside forces - including the failure to promote oneself. The act of self-promotion cannot, by definition, dehumanize the narcissist or humiliate him. In a Total Institution (or in a Total Situation) the narcissist is no longer a human being - he has nothing.

The positive aspect of total situations is that the narcissist is rendered special and mysterious by virtue of being a stranger and even by the enigma of his prior identity. The narcissist cannot envy the natives' successes and happiness - clearly they had a head start. They belong, they control, they dictate, they are supported by social networks and codes.

The narcissist cannot accept that anyone is more knowledgeable than he is. He is likely to argue vehemently with the medical staff attending him over his treatment, for instance. But he succumbs to force (the more brutal and explicit - the better). And while doing so, the narcissist feels a great relief: the race is over and responsibility has been shifted to the outside. He is almost euphoric when relieved of the need to make decisions, or when he finds himself in a bad spot because this vindicates his internal voices, which keep telling him that he is bad and should be punished.

It is this fear of failure - especially the fear of failing to promote himself - that thwarts the narcissist's relationships with women and with other figures of authority or of import in his life.

It is really the old fear of being abandoned in one of its endless guises. The narcissist envies his deserting partner. He knows how difficult and emotionally wrenching it is to live with him. He realizes that his partner will be much better off without him - and this makes him sad (that he was unable to offer her an acceptable alternative) and envious (that her lot is likely to be better than his.) Of course, he displaces some of his emotions, blaming his partner, then blaming himself, angry at her and afraid to feel this (forbidden) anger (at his mother's substitute).

The narcissist does not feel sorry because a specific individual - his partner - abandoned him. He feels sorry because he was abandoned. It is the act of abandonment, which matters - the abandoning figures (his mother, his partners) are interchangeable.

The narcissist always shares his life with a fantasy, an idealization, with an ideal phantasm he imposes upon his real life partner. Abandonment is only the rebellion of the real life partner against this fiction invented and compulsively enforced by the narcissist, against the humiliation thus suffered - verbal and behavioral.

For the narcissist, to be abandoned means to be judged and found wanting. To be deserted means to be deemed replaceable. At its extreme, it can come to mean the emotional annihilation of the narcissist. He feels that when a woman leaves him she does so because there it is emotionally easy to get away from him and never to see him again. There is no problem to bid farewell to someone who just is not there (at least emotionally). The narcissist feels annulled, rendered transparent, abused, exploited, and objectified.

Put differently, the narcissist experiences through abandonment (even through the mere risk of abandonment) a re-enactment of the very mistreatment and abuses, which, earlier in his life, transformed him into the deformed creature that he is. He gets a taste of the medicine (rather poison) that he often ruthlessly administers to others. At the same time he relives his harrowing childhood experiences.

This mirror matrix of forces is too much for the narcissist to bear. He begins to disintegrate and veers into utter and complete dysfunction. At this late stage, he is likely to entertain suicidal ideation. An encounter with the opposite sex holds mortal risks for the narcissist - more ominous than the risks normally associated with it.

The Spouse / Mate / Partner of the Narcissist

The narcissist's mate or spouse may be a warm, independent woman – but she may also be a codependent or an inverted narcissist.

The narcissist abuses his intimate partner in numerous ways: overtly, covertly, by being unpredictable, reacting disproportionately, dehumanizing, objectifying, and leveraging personal information.

He may also use ambient abuse (gaslighting) or abuse her by proxy, via third parties.

Question:

What kind of a spouse/mate/partner is likely to be attracted to a narcissist, or to attract a narcissist?

Answer:

The Victims

On the face of it, there is no (emotional) partner or mate, who typically "binds" with a narcissist. They come in all shapes and sizes. The initial phases of attraction, infatuation and falling in love are pretty normal. The narcissist puts on his best face – the other party is blinded by budding love. A natural selection process occurs only much later, as the relationship develops and is put to the test.

Living with a narcissist can be exhilarating, is always onerous, often harrowing. Surviving a relationship with a narcissist indicates, therefore, the parameters of the personality of the survivor. She (or, more rarely, he) is moulded by the relationship into The Typical Narcissistic Mate/Partner/Spouse.

First and foremost, the narcissist's partner must have a deficient or a distorted grasp of her self and of reality. Otherwise, she (or he) is bound to abandon the narcissist's ship early on. The cognitive distortion is likely to consist of belittling and demeaning herself – while aggrandising and adoring the narcissist.

The partner is, thus, placing herself in the position of the eternal victim: undeserving, punishable, a scapegoat. Sometimes, it is very important to the partner to appear moral, sacrificial and victimised. At other times, she is not even aware of this predicament. The narcissist is perceived by the partner to be a person in the position to demand these sacrifices from her because he is superior in many ways (intellectually, emotionally, morally, professionally, or financially).

The status of professional victim sits well with the partner's tendency to punish herself, namely: with her masochistic streak. The tormented life with the narcissist is just what she deserves.

In this respect, the partner is the mirror image of the narcissist. By maintaining a symbiotic relationship with him, by being totally dependent upon her source of masochistic supply (which the narcissist most reliably constitutes and most amply provides) the partner enhances certain traits and encourages certain behaviours, which are at the very core of narcissism.

The narcissist is never whole without an adoring, submissive, available, self-denigrating partner. His very sense of superiority, indeed his False Self, depends on it. His sadistic Superego switches its attentions from the narcissist (in whom it often provokes suicidal ideation) to the partner, thus finally obtaining an alternative source of sadistic satisfaction.

It is through self-denial that the partner survives. She denies her wishes, hopes, dreams, aspirations, sexual, psychological and material needs, choices, preferences, values, and much else besides. She perceives her needs as threatening because they might engender the wrath of the narcissist's God-like supreme figure.

The narcissist is rendered in her eyes even more superior through and because of this self-denial. Self-denial undertaken to facilitate and ease the life of a "great man" is more palatable. The "greater" the man (=the narcissist), the easier it is for the partner to ignore her own self, to dwindle, to degenerate, to turn into an appendix of the narcissist and, finally, to become nothing but an extension, to merge with the narcissist to the point of oblivion and of merely dim memories of herself.

The two collaborate in this macabre dance. The narcissist is formed by his partner inasmuch as he forms her. Submission breeds superiority and masochism breeds sadism. The relationships are characterised by emergentism: roles are allocated almost from the start and any deviation meets with an aggressive, even violent reaction.

The predominant state of the partner's mind is utter confusion. Even the most basic relationships – with husband, children, or parents – remain bafflingly obscured by the giant shadow cast by the intensive interaction with the narcissist. A suspension of judgement is part and parcel of a suspension of individuality, which is both a prerequisite to and the result of living with a narcissist. The partner no longer knows what is true and right and what is wrong and forbidden.

The narcissist recreates for the partner the sort of emotional ambience that led to his own formation in the first place: capriciousness, fickleness, arbitrariness, emotional (and physical or sexual) abandonment. The world becomes hostile, and ominous and the partner has only one thing left to cling to: the narcissist.

And cling she does. If there is anything which can safely be said about those who emotionally team up with narcissists, it is that they are overtly and overly dependent.

The partner doesn't know what to do – and this is only too natural in the mayhem that is the relationship with the narcissist. But the typical partner also does not know what she wants and, to a large extent, who she is and what she wishes to become.

These unanswered questions hamper the partner's ability to gauge reality. Her primordial sin is that she fell in love with an image, not with a real person. It is the voiding of the image that is mourned when the relationship ends.

The break-up of a relationship with a narcissist is, therefore, very emotionally charged. It is the culmination of a long chain of humiliations and of subjugation. It is the rebellion of the functioning and healthy parts of the partner's personality against the tyranny of the narcissist.

The partner is likely to have totally misread and misinterpreted the whole interaction (I hesitate to call it a relationship). This lack of proper interface with reality might be (erroneously) labelled "pathological".

Why is it that the partner seeks to prolong her pain? What is the source and purpose of this masochistic streak? Upon the break-up of the relationship, the partner (but not the narcissist, who usually refuses to provide closure) engages in a tortuous and drawn out post mortem.

Sometimes, the breakup is initiated by the long-suffering spouse or intimate partner. As she develops and matures, gaining in self-confidence and a modicum of self-esteem (ironically, at the narcissist's behest in his capacity as her "guru" and "father figure"), she acquires more personal autonomy and refuses to cater to the energy-draining neediness of her narcissist: she no longer provides him with all-important secondary narcissistic supply (ostentatious respect, owe, adulation, undivided attention admiration, and the rehashed memories of past successes and triumphs.)

Typically, the roles are then reversed and the narcissist displays codependent behaviors, such as clinging, in a desperate attempt to hang-on to his "creation", his hitherto veteran and reliable source of quality supply. These are further exacerbated by the ageing narcissist's increasing social isolation, psychological disintegration (decompensation), andrecurrent failures and defeats.

But the question who did what to whom (and even why) is irrelevant. What is relevant is to stop mourning oneself, start smiling again and love in a less subservient, hopeless, and pain-inflicting manner.

A cerebral narcissist wrote this to me (in parentheses, my comments, signed SV):

Click HERE to Watch the Video

"I guess I am a throwback to the men of the 18th or 19th century: patriarchal and transactional (compare this statement to findings by Keller et al. - SV) I have had several serious relationships, including one engagement to be married and three marriages.

The pattern had always been the same: having selected a woman far inferior to my position in life (and, thus, less likely to abandon ship) and following a brief period of rampant sex (to demonstrate to her that I am 'normal' and to make her look forward to years of great physical and emotional intimacy – false advertising, I admit), I subside into this recluse, interested only in my studies, reading, writing, and the universe of the mind. Zero sex, no love, no intimacy, physical or emotional, no children, no home (always lived in rented flats), and no family. Take it or leave it and minimal nuisance value.

Her roles are: (1) to admire me; (2) to remind me of my past accomplishments and 'glory'; (3) to act as a glorified housemaid and do the chores; (4) to serve as my companion, available on the spur of the moment to do my bidding and adhere to my plans and decisions; (5) to reflect well on me by not shaming me in public with her ignorance, promiscuity, or idleness.

As long as she fulfilled the aforementioned functions, I didn't really care what else she did with her time and with whom. Nothing stirred in me, not even a hint of jealousy, when all my women told me that they had cheated on me with other men, some of them multiply. But, when they showed clear signs of bolting, when they became disenchanted, bitterly disappointed, disaffected, disillusioned, cold, aloof, weary, demonstratively absent, lost all interest in me and my work, verbally and psychologically abused me, and refused to do things together anymore, I panicked because I was afraid to lose their valued services.

I dreaded the time, effort, and resources required to 'break in', train, 'domesticate', and habituate another woman to my needs and particular requirements (convert them to sources of secondary narcissistic supply - SV.) I was also tired of having my women abscond with half my assets time and again. After all: I only married them only to secure their presence in my life and I did provide them with a lifestyle which they could never have attained by themselves, inferior as they were to start with!

Faced with such a daunting prospect, I embarked on a charm offensive and I again offered them sex, intimacy, love, attention, and, if needed, adulation. Only, usually, at this stage, it was too late and definitely too little. She was already far-gone. She bolted all the same.

All my women felt that something was wrong with me, that something was missing in the relationship such as it was, but they couldn't quite place their collective finger on it. I simply absented myself because I regarded full-fledged intimate relationships as both a colossal waste of my precious time and the manifestation of socially-sanctioned mediocrity. There had always been a discrepancy in expectations which led to inevitable breakups and acrimony."

Click HERE to Watch the Video

The Abuse

Abuse is an integral, inseparable part of the Narcissistic Personality Disorder.

The narcissist idealises and then **_DEVALUES_** and discards the object of his initial idealisation. This abrupt, heartless devaluation **_IS_** abuse. **_ALL_** narcissists idealise and then devalue. This is **THE** core narcissistic behaviour. The narcissist exploits, lies, insults, demeans, ignores (the "silent treatment"), manipulates, controls. All these are forms of abuse.

There are a million ways to abuse. To love too much is to abuse. It is tantamount to treating someone as one's extension, an object, or an instrument of gratification. To be over-protective, not to respect privacy, to be brutally honest, with a morbid sense of humour, or consistently tactless – is to abuse. To expect too much, to denigrate, to ignore – are all modes of abuse. There is physical abuse, verbal abuse, psychological abuse, sexual abuse. The list is long.

Narcissists are masters of abusing surreptitiously ("ambient abuse"). They are "stealth abusers". You have to actually live with one in order to witness the abuse.

There are three important categories of abuse:

1. **Overt Abuse** – The open and explicit abuse of another person. Threatening, coercing, battering, lying, berating, demeaning, chastising, insulting, humiliating, exploiting, ignoring ("silent treatment"), devaluing, unceremoniously discarding, verbal abuse, physical abuse and sexual abuse are all forms of overt abuse.
2. **Covert or Controlling Abuse** – Narcissism is almost entirely about control. It is a primitive and immature reaction to the circumstances of a life in which the narcissist (usually in his childhood) was rendered helpless. It is about re-asserting one's identity, re-establishing predictability, mastering the environment – human and physical.
3. The bulk of narcissistic behaviours can be traced to this panicky reaction to the potential for loss of control. Narcissists are hypochondriacs (and difficult patients) because they are afraid to lose control over their body, its looks and its proper functioning. They are obsessive-compulsive in their efforts to subdue their physical habitat and render it foreseeable. They stalk people and harass them as a means of "being in touch" – another form of narcissistic control.

But why the panic?

The narcissist is a solipsist. To him, nothing exists except himself. Meaningful others are his extensions, assimilated by him, they are internal objects – not external ones. Thus, losing control of a significant other is equivalent to losing the use of a limb, or of one's brain. It is terrifying.

Independent or disobedient people evoke in the narcissist the realisation that something is wrong with his worldview, that he is not the centre of the world or its cause and that he cannot control what, to him, are internal representations.

To the narcissist, losing control means going insane. Because other people are mere elements in the narcissist's mind – being unable to manipulate them literally means losing it (his mind). Imagine, if you suddenly were to find out that you cannot manipulate your memories or control your thoughts… Nightmarish!

Moreover, it is often only through manipulation and extortion that the narcissist can secure his Narcissistic Supply (NS). Controlling his Sources of Narcissistic Supply is a (mental) life or death question for the narcissist. The narcissist is a drug addict (his drug being the NS) and he would go to any length to obtain the next dose.

In his frantic efforts to maintain control or re-assert it, the narcissist resorts to a myriad of fiendishly inventive stratagems and mechanisms. Here is a partial list:

Unpredictability

The narcissist acts unpredictably, capriciously, inconsistently and irrationally. This serves to demolish in others their carefully crafted worldview. They become dependent upon the next twist and turn of the narcissist, his inexplicable whims, his outbursts, denial, or smiles.

In other words: the narcissist makes sure that **HE** is the only stable entity in the lives of others – by shattering the rest of their world through his seemingly insane behaviour. He guarantees his presence in their lives – by destabilising them.

In the absence of a self, there are no likes or dislikes, preferences, predictable behaviour or characteristics. It is not possible to know the narcissist. There is no one there.

The narcissist was conditioned – from an early age of abuse and trauma – to expect the unexpected. His was a world in which (sometimes sadistic) capricious caretakers and peers often behaved arbitrarily. He was trained to deny his True Self and nurture a False one.

Having invented himself, the narcissist sees no problem in re-inventing that which he designed in the first place. The narcissist is his own creator.

Hence his grandiosity.

Moreover, the narcissist is a man for all seasons, forever adaptable, constantly imitating and emulating, a human sponge, a perfect mirror, a chameleon, a non-entity that is, at the same time, all entities combined. The narcissist is best described by Heidegger's phrase: "Being and Nothingness". Into this reflective vacuum, this sucking black hole, the narcissist attracts the Sources of his Narcissistic Supply.

To an observer, the narcissist appears to be fractured or discontinuous.

Pathological narcissism has been compared to the Dissociative Identity Disorder (formerly the Multiple Personality Disorder). By definition, the narcissist has at least two selves, the True and False ones. His personality is very primitive and disorganised. Living with a narcissist is a nauseating experience not only because of what he is – but because of what he is **NOT**. He is not a fully formed human – but a dizzyingly kaleidoscopic gallery of ephemeral images, which melt into each other seamlessly. It is incredibly disorienting.

It is also exceedingly problematic. Promises made by the narcissist are easily disowned by him. His plans are transient. His emotional ties – a simulacrum. Most narcissists have one island of stability in their life (spouse, family, their career, a hobby, their religion, country, or idol) – pounded by the turbulent currents of a dishevelled existence.

The narcissist does not keep agreements, does not adhere to laws or social norms, and regards consistency and predictability as demeaning traits.

Thus, to invest in a narcissist is a purposeless, futile and meaningless activity. To the narcissist, every day is a new beginning, a hunt, a new cycle of idealisation or devaluation, a newly invented self. There is no accumulation of credits or goodwill because the narcissist has no past and no future. He occupies an eternal and timeless present. He is a fossil caught in the frozen ashes of a volcanic childhood.

TIP

Refuse to accept such behaviour. Demand reasonably predictable and rational actions and reactions. Insist on respect for your boundaries, predilections, preferences, and priorities.

Disproportional Reactions

One of the favourite tools of manipulation in the narcissist's arsenal is the disproportionality of his reactions. He reacts with supreme rage to the slightest slight. He punishes severely for what he perceives to be an offence against him, no matter how minor. He throws a temper tantrum over any discord or disagreement, however gently and considerately expressed. Or he may act attentive, charming and seductive (even over-sexed, if need be). This ever-shifting emotional landscape ("affective dunes") coupled with an inordinately harsh and arbitrarily applied "penal code" are both promulgated by the narcissist. Neediness and dependence on the source of all justice meted – on the narcissist – are thus guaranteed.

TIP

Demand a just and proportional treatment. Reject or ignore unjust and capricious behaviour.

If you are up to the inevitable confrontation, react in kind. Let him taste some of his own medicine.

Dehumanization and Objectification

People have a need to believe in the empathic skills and basic good-heartedness of others. By dehumanising and objectifying people – the narcissist attacks the very foundations of the social treaty. This is the "alien" aspect of narcissists – they may be excellent imitations of fully formed adults but they are emotionally non-existent, or, at best, immature.

This is so horrid, so repulsive, so phantasmagoric – that people recoil in terror. It is then, with their defences absolutely down, that they are the most susceptible and vulnerable to the narcissist's control. Physical, psychological, verbal and sexual abuse are all forms of dehumanisation and objectification.

TIP

Never show your abuser that you are afraid of him. Do not negotiate with bullies. They are insatiable. Do not succumb to blackmail.

If things get rough- disengage, involve law enforcement officers, friends and colleagues, or threaten him (legally).

Do not keep your abuse a secret. Secrecy is the abuser's weapon.

Never give him a second chance. React with your full arsenal to the first transgression.

Abuse of Information

From the first moments of an encounter with another person, the narcissist is on the prowl. He collects information with the intention of applying it later to extract Narcissistic Supply. The more he knows about his potential Source of Supply – the better able he is to coerce, manipulate, charm, extort or convert it "to the cause". The narcissist does not hesitate to abuse the information he gleaned, regardless of its intimate nature or the circumstances in which he obtained it. This is a powerful tool in his armoury.

TIP

Be guarded. Don't be too forthcoming in a first or casual meeting. Gather intelligence.

Be yourself. Don't misrepresent your wishes, boundaries, preferences, priorities, and red lines.

Do not behave inconsistently. Do not go back on your word. Be firm and resolute.

Impossible Situations

The narcissist engineers impossible, dangerous, unpredictable, unprecedented, or highly specific situations in which he is sorely and indispensably needed. The narcissist, his knowledge, his skills or his traits become the only ones applicable, or the most useful to coping with these artificial predicaments. It is a form of control by proxy.

TIP

Stay away from such quagmires. Scrutinize every offer and suggestion, no matter how innocuous.

Prepare backup plans. Keep others informed of your whereabouts and appraised of your situation.

Be vigilant and doubting. Do not be gullible and suggestible. Better safe than sorry.

Control by Proxy

If all else fails, the narcissist recruits friends, colleagues, mates, family members, the authorities, institutions, neighbours, or the media – in short, third parties – to do his bidding. He uses them to cajole, coerce, threaten, stalk, offer, retreat, tempt, convince, harass, communicate and otherwise manipulate his target. He controls these unaware instruments exactly as he plans to control his ultimate prey. He employs the same mechanisms and devices. And he dumps his props unceremoniously when the job is done.

Another form of control by proxy is to engineer situations in which abuse is inflicted upon another person. Such carefully crafted scenarios involve embarrassment and humiliation as well as social sanctions (condemnation, opprobrium, or even physical punishment). Society, or a social group become the instruments of the narcissist.

TIP

Often the abuser's proxies are unaware of their role. Expose him. Inform them. Demonstrate to them how they are being abused, misused, and plain used by the abuser.

Trap your abuser. Treat him as he treats you. Involve others. Bring it into the open. Nothing like sunshine to disinfest abuse.

Ambient Abuse

The fostering, propagation and enhancement of an atmosphere of fear, intimidation, instability, unpredictability and irritation. There are no acts of traceable or provable explicit abuse, nor any manipulative settings of control. Yet, the irksome feeling remains, a disagreeable foreboding, a premonition, a bad omen. This is sometimes called "gaslighting".

In the long-term, such an environment erodes one's sense of self-worth and self-esteem. Self-confidence is shaken badly. Often, the victims go a paranoid or schizoid and thus are exposed even more to criticism and judgement. The roles are thus reversed: the victim is considered mentally disordered and the narcissist – the suffering soul or the victim.

TIP

Run! Get away! Ambient abuse often develops into overt and violent abuse.

You don't owe anyone an explanation – but you owe yourself a life. Bail out of the relationship.

The Malignant Optimism of the Abused

I often come across sad examples of the powers of self-delusion that the narcissist provokes in his victims. It is what I call "malignant optimism". People refuse to believe that some questions are unsolvable, some diseases incurable, some disasters inevitable. They see a sign of hope in every fluctuation. They read meaning and patterns into every random occurrence, utterance, or slip. They are deceived by their own pressing need to believe in the ultimate victory of good over evil, health over sickness, order over disorder. Life appears otherwise so meaningless, so unjust and so arbitrary…

So, they impose upon it a design, progress, aims, and paths. This is magical thinking.

"If only he tried hard enough", "If he only really wanted to heal", "If only we found the right therapy", "If only his defences were down", "There **MUST** be something good and worthy under the hideous facade", "**NO ONE** can be that evil and destructive", "He must have meant it differently", "God, or a higher being, or the spirit, or the soul is the solution and the answer to our prayers", "He is not responsible for what he is - his narcissism is the product of a difficult childhood, of abuse, and of his monstrous parents."

The Pollyanna defences of the abused are aimed against the emerging and horrible understanding that humans are mere specks of dust in a totally indifferent universe, the playthings of evil and sadistic forces, of which the narcissist is one - and that finally their pain means nothing to anyone but themselves. Nothing whatsoever. It has all been in vain.

The narcissist holds such thinking in barely undisguised contempt. To him, it is a sign of weakness, the scent of prey, a gaping vulnerability. He uses and abuses this human need for order, good, and meaning – as he uses and abuses all other human needs. Gullibility, selective blindness, malignant optimism – these are the weapons of the beast. And the abused are hard at work to provide it with its arsenal.

Codependence and Dependent Personality Disorder

There is great confusion regarding the terms co-dependent, counter-dependent, and dependent. Before we proceed to study the Dependent Personality Disorder in our next article, we would do well to clarify these terms.

Codependents

Like dependents (people with the Dependent Personality Disorder), codependents depend on other people for their emotional gratification and the performance of both inconsequential and crucial daily and psychological functions.

Codependents are needy, demanding, and submissive. They suffer from abandonment anxiety and, to avoid being overwhelmed by it, they cling to others and act immaturely. These behaviours are intended to elicit protective responses and to safeguard the "relationship" with their companion or mate upon whom they depend. Codependents appear to be impervious to abuse. No matter how badly mistreated, they remain committed.

This is where the "co" in "co-dependence" comes into play. By accepting the role of victims, codependents seek to control their abusers and manipulate them. It is a danse macabre in which both members of the dyad collaborate.

The codependent sometimes claims to pity her abuser and cast herself in the grandiose roles of his saviour and redeemer. Her overwhelming empathy imprisons the codependent in these dysfunctional relationships and she feels guilt either because she believes that she had driven the abuser to maltreat her or because she contemplates abandoning him.

Typology of Codependents

Codependence is a complex, multi-faceted, and multi-dimensional defence against the codependent's fears and needs. There are four categories of codependence, stemming from their respective aetiologies:

(i) Codependence that aims to fend of anxieties related to abandonment. These codependents are clingy, smothering, and prone to panic, are plagued with ideas of reference, and display self-negating submissiveness. Their main concern is to prevent their victims (friends, spouses, family members) from deserting them or from attaining true autonomy and independence. These codependents merge with their "loved" ones and experience any sign of abandonment (actual, threatened, or even imagined) as a form of self-annihilation or "amputation".

(ii) Codependence that is geared to cope with the codependent's fear of losing control. By feigning helplessness and neediness such codependents coerce their environment into ceaselessly catering to their needs, wishes, and requirements. These codependents are "drama queens" and their life is a kaleidoscope of instability and chaos. They refuse to grow up and force their nearest and dearest to treat them as emotional and/or physical invalids. They deploy their self-imputed deficiencies and disabilities as weapons.

Both these types of codependents use emotional blackmail and, when necessary, threats to secure the presence and blind compliance of their "suppliers".

(iii) Vicarious codependents live through others. They "sacrifice" themselves in order to glory in the accomplishments of their chosen targets. They subsist on reflected light, on second-hand applause, and on derivative achievements. They have no personal history, having suspended their wishes, preferences, and dreams in favour of another's.

From my book "Malignant Self Love - Narcissism Revisited":

"Inverted Narcissist

Also called "covert narcissist", this is a co-dependent who depends exclusively on narcissists (narcissist-co-dependent). If you are living with a narcissist, have a relationship with one, if you are married to one, if you are working with a narcissist, etc. – it does NOT mean that you are an inverted narcissist.

To "qualify" as an inverted narcissist, you must CRAVE to be in a relationship with a narcissist, regardless of any abuse inflicted on you by him/her. You must ACTIVELY seek relationships with narcissists and ONLY with narcissists, no matter what your (bitter and traumatic) past experience has been. You must feel EMPTY and UNHAPPY in relationships with ANY OTHER kind of person. Only then, and if you satisfy the other diagnostic criteria of a Dependent Personality Disorder, can you be safely labelled an 'inverted narcissist'."

(iv) "**Codependent or Borderline narcissists**" oscillate between periods of clinging and other codependent behavior patterns (which they interpret as "intimacy") and eras of aloofness, detachment, and emotional neglect and abandonment (which they regard as legitimate and the only possible manifestations of their personal autonomy and space.) They also tend to form with their intimate partner a shared psychosis. These are all the outcomes of their overwhelming and all-pervasive abandonment anxiety: they either smother their partner in an attempt to forestall desertion – or they pre-emptively abandon ship, thus avoiding hurt and maintaining an illusion of control over the situation ("I walked out on her and dumped her, not the other way around.")

The codependent deploys strategies such as merger (becoming one with her intimate partner while renouncing all personal autonomy and independence of both of them, up to a point of shared psychosis); coextensivity (the "ventriloquist defense": insisting that the partner mind-reads her and acts in ways that reflect her inner psychological states and moods); and shifting boundaries (using behavioural unpredictability and ambient uncertainty to induce paralysing dependence in the partner.)

(v) Finally, there is another form of dependence that is so subtle that it eluded detection until very recently.

Counterdependents

Counterdependents reject and despise authority and often clash with authority figures (parents, boss, the Law). Their sense of self-worth and their very self-identity are premised on and derived from (in other words, are dependent on) these acts of bravura and defiance. They are "personal autonomy militants". Counterdependents are fiercely, militantly independent; controlling; self-centered; and aggressive. Many of them are antisocial and use Projective Identification (i.e. force people to behave in ways that buttresses and affirm the counterdependent's view of the world and his expectations).

These behavior patterns are often the result of a deep-seated fear of intimacy. In an intimate relationship, the counterdependent feels enslaved, ensnared, and captive. Counterdependents are locked into "approach-avoidance repetition complex" cycles. Hesitant approach is followed by avoidance of commitment. They are "lone wolves" and bad team players.

From my book "Malignant Self Love - Narcissism Revisited":

"Counterdependence is a reaction formation. The counterdependent dreads his own weaknesses. He seeks to overcome them by projecting an image of omnipotence, omniscience, success, self-sufficiency, and superiority.

Most "classical" (overt) narcissists are counterdependent. Their emotions and needs are buried under "scar tissue" which had formed, coalesced, and hardened during years of one form of abuse or another. Grandiosity, a sense of entitlement, a lack of empathy, and overweening haughtiness usually hide gnawing insecurity and a fluctuating sense of self-worth."

The Dependent Personality Disorder is a much disputed mental health diagnosis.

We are all dependent to some degree. We all like to be taken care of. When is this need judged to be pathological, compulsive, pervasive, and excessive? Clinicians who contributed to the study of this disorder use words such as "craving", "clinging", "stifling" (both the dependent and her partner), and "humiliating", or "submissive". But these are all subjective terms, open to disagreement and differences of opinion.

Moreover, virtually all cultures encourage dependency to varying degrees. Even in developed countries, many women, the very old, the very young, the sick, the criminal, and the mentally-handicapped are denied personal autonomy and are legally and economically dependent on others (or on the authorities). Thus, the Dependent Personality Disorder is diagnosed only when such behavior does not conform to social or cultural norms.

Codependents, as they are sometimes known, are possessed with fantastic worries and concerns and are paralyzed by their abandonment anxiety and fear of separation. This inner turmoil renders them indecisive. Even the simplest everyday decision becomes an excruciating ordeal. This is why codependents rarely initiate projects or do things on their own.

Dependents typically go around eliciting constant and repeated reassurances and advice from myriad sources. This recurrent solicitation of succour is proof that the codependent seeks to transfer responsibility for his or her life to others, whether they have agreed to assume it or not.

This recoil and studious avoidance of challenges may give the wrong impression that the Dependent is indolent or insipid. Yet, most Dependents are neither. They are often fired by repressed ambition, energy, and imagination. It is their lack self-confidence that holds them back. They don't trust their own abilities and judgment.

Absent an inner compass and a realistic assessment of their positive qualities on the one hand and limitations on the other hand, Dependents are forced to rely on crucial input from the outside. Realizing this, their behavior becomes self-negating: they never disagree with meaningful others or criticizes them. They are afraid to lose their support and emotional nurturance.

Consequently, as I have written in the Open Site Encyclopedia entry on this disorder:

"The codependent moulds himself/herself and bends over backward to cater to the needs of his nearest and dearest and satisfy their every whim, wish, expectation, and demand. Nothing is too unpleasant or unacceptable if it serves to secure the uninterrupted presence of the codependent's family and friends and the emotional sustenance s/he can extract (or extort) from them.

The codependent does not feel fully alive when alone. S/he feels helpless, threatened, ill-at-ease, and child-like. This acute discomfort drives the codependent to hop from one relationship to another. The sources of nurturance are interchangeable. To the codependent, being with someone, with anyone, no matter who, is always preferable to solitude."

Read Notes from the therapy of a Dependent (Codependent) Patient

The Codependent's Inner Mother and Child

Parents of codependents teach their offspring to expect only conditional, transactional love: the child is supposed to render a service or fulfil the parent's wishes in return for affection and compassion, attention and emotion. Ineluctably, the hurt child reacts with rage to this unjust mistreatment.

With no recourse to the offending parent, this fury is either directed outwardly, at others (who stand in for the bad parent) - or inwardly. The former solution yields a psychopath, or a passive-aggressive (negativistic) - the latter solution, a masochist. Similarly, with an unavailable parent, the child's reserve of love can be directed inward, at himself (to yield a narcissist), or outward, towards others (and, thus, form a codependent.)

All these choices retard personal growth and are self-annihilating. In all four paths the adult plays the dual roles of a punitive parent and an eternal child, who is unable and unwilling to grow up for fear of incurring the wrath of the parent with whom he had merged so thoroughly early on.

When the codependent merges with a love object, she interprets her newfound attachment and bond as a betrayal of the punitive parent. She fully anticipates the internalized parent's disapproval and dreads its (self-)destructive disciplinarian measures. In an attempt to placate this implacable divinity she turns on her partner and lashes out at him, thus establishing where her true loyalties and affiliation lie (i.e., with the parent.) Concurrently, she punishes herself as she tries to pre-empt the merciless onslaught of her sadistic parental introjects and superego: she engages in a panoply of self-destructive and self-defeating behaviours.

Acutely aware of the risk of losing her partner owing to her abusive misconduct, the codependent experiences extreme abandonment anxiety. She swings wildly between self-effacing and clinging ("doormat") behaviours on the one hand and explosive, vituperative invective on the other hand: the former being the manifestations of her "eternal child" and the latter expressions of her "punitive parent".

Such abrupt shifts in affect and conduct are often misdiagnosed as the hallmarks of a mood disorder, especially Bipolar Disorder. But where Dependent Personality Disorder is diagnosed, these pendular tectonic upheavals are indicative of an underlying personality structure rather than of any biochemically-induced perturbations.

"I Can't Live Without Him/Her"

Click HERE to watch the video

Akin to addiction, dependence on other people fulfils important mental health functions. First, it is an organizing principle: it serves to explain behaviours and events within a coherent "narrative" (fictional story) or frame of reference ("I acted this way because ..."). Second, it gives meaning to life. Third: the constant ups and downs satisfy your need for excitement and thrills. Fourth, and most crucially, your addiction and emotional lability place you at the center of attention and allow you to manipulate people around you to do your bidding.

Indeed, you are convinced that you cannot live without your dependence.

This is a subtle and important distinction: you can survive without him or her, but you believe profoundly (erroneously as it happens) that you cannot go on living without your addiction to your partner. You experience your dependence as your best friend, your comfort zone, as familiar and warm and fitting as an old pair of slippers. You are addicted to and dependent on your dependence, but you attribute its source to boyfriends, mates, spouses, children, parents - anyone who happens to fit the bill and the plot of your narrative. They come and go - your addiction remains intact; they are interchangeable - your dependence is immutable.

So, what can you do about it?

Extreme cases of codependence (such as Dependent or Borderline Personality Disorders) require professional help. Luckily, dependence is a spectrum and most people with dependent traits and behaviours are clustered somewhere in the middle. Help yourself by realizing that the world never comes to end when relationships do: it is your dependence which reacts with desperation, not you. Next, analyze your addiction: what are the stories and narratives that underlie it? Do you tend to idealize your intimate partner? If so, can you see him or her in a more realistic light? Are you anxious about being abandoned? Why? Have you been traumatically abandoned in the past, as a child, perhaps? Write down the worst possible scenario: the relationship is over and s/he leaves you. Is your physical survival at stake? Of course not. Make a list of the consequences of the breakup and write, next to each one what you can and intend to do about it. Armed with this plan of action, you are bound to feel safer and more confident.

Finally, make sure to share your thoughts, fears, and emotions with friends and family. Social support is indispensable. One good friend is worth a hundred therapy sessions.

Countering Abandonment and Separation Anxiety

Click HERE to Watch the Video

Clinging and smothering behaviours are the unsavoury consequences of a deep-set existential, almost mortal fear of abandonment and separation. For the codependent to maintain a long-term, healthy relationship, she must first confront her anxieties head on. This can be done via psychotherapy: the therapeutic alliance is a contract between patient and therapist which provides for a safe environment, where abandonment is not an option and, thus, where the client can resume personal growth and form a modicum of self-autonomy. In extremis, a psychiatrist may wish to prescribe anti-anxiety medication.

Self-help is also an option, though; meditation, yoga, and the elimination of any and all addictions, such as workaholism, or binge eating. Feelings of emptiness and loneliness – at the core of abandonment anxiety and other dysfunctional attachment styles – can be countered with meaningful activities (mainly altruistic and charitable) and true, stable friends, who provide a safe haven and are unlikely to abandon her and, therefore, constitute a holding, supportive, and nourishing environment.

The codependent's reflexive responses to her inner turmoil are self-defeating and counterproductive. They often bring about the very outcomes she fears most. But these outcomes also tend to buttress her worldview ("the world is hostile, I am bound to get hurt") and sustain her comfort zone ("abuse and abandonment are familiar to me; at least I know the ropes and how to cope with them.")

This is why she needs to exit this realm of mirrored fears and fearsome mental tumult. She should adopt new avocations and hobbies, meet new people, engage is non-committal, dispensable relationships, and, in general, take life more lightly.

Some codependents develop a type of "militant independence" as a defense against their own sorely felt vulnerability (their dependence.) But even these daring "rebels" tend to view their relationships in terms of "black and white" (an infantile psychological defense mechanism known as "splitting".) They tend to regard their relationships as either doomed to failure or everlasting and their mates as both unique and indispensable ("soulmate", "twin") or completely interchangeable (objectified.)

These, of course, are misperceptions; cognitive deficits grounded in emotional immaturity and thwarted personal development. All relationships have a life expectancy, a "sell by", "good before", or expiry date. No one is irreplaceable or completely interchangeable. The codependent's problems are rooted in a profound lack of self-love and an absence of object constancy (she regards herself as unloved and unlovable when she is all by herself.)

Yet, clinging, codependent, and counterdependent (fiercely independent, defiant, and intimacy-retarding) behaviours can be modified. If you fear abandonment to the point of a phobia, here's my advice:

Compile a written, very detailed "mission statement" regarding all the aspects of your romantic relationships: how would you like them to look like and how would you go about securing the best outcomes. Revisit and revise this "charter" regularly.

List your 3 most important mate choice criteria: what would you be looking for in a first date and without which there will be no second date. This list is your filter, your proverbial selective membrane. Revisit and revise it regularly as your taste and preferences change.

Conduct a thorough background check on your prospective intimate partner. Go online and Google his name; visit his social networking accounts; ask friends and family for information and an appraisal of his character, temperament, and personality. This preparatory research will put you in control and empower you. It will serve as an antidote to uncertainty and the anxiety attendant upon it.

Next use the "Volatility Threshold" and the "Threat Monitoring" tools.

The "Volatility Threshold" instrument is a compilation of 1-3 types of behaviours that you consider critically desirable ("deal-makers") in your partner. Observe him and add up the number of times he had acted inconsistently and, thus, reversed these crucial aspects of his behavior substantially and essentially. Decide in advance how many "strikes" would constitute a "deal-breaker" and when he reaches this number – simply leave. Do not share with him either the existence or the content of this "test" lest it might affect his performance and cause him to playact and prevaricate.

As a codependent, you tend to jump to conclusions and then "jump the gun": you greatly exaggerate the significance of even minor infractions and disagreements and you are always unduly fatalistic and pessimistic about the survival chances of your relationships. The "Threat Monitoring" tool is comprised of an inventory of warning signs and red flags that, in your view and from your experience, herald and portend abandonment. The aim is to falsify this list: to prove to you that, more often than not, you are wrong in predicting a breakup.

In general, try to act as though you were a scientist: construct alternative hypotheses (interpretations of behaviours and events) to account for what you regard as transgressions and bad omens. Test these hypotheses before you decide to end it all with a grand gesture, a dramatic exit, or a decisive finale. Preemptive abandonment is based more on your insecurities than on facts, so make sure to test your hypotheses – and your partner - in a variety of settings before you call it a day and before you prophesy doom and gloom.

This "scientific" approach to your intimate relationship has the added benefit of delaying the instant alleviation of your anxiety which consists of impulsive, ill-thought actions. It takes time to form hypotheses and test them. This lapse between trigger and reaction is all you need. By the time you have formed your informed opinion, your anxiety will have abated and you will no longer feel the urge to "do something now, whatever it may be!"

Armed with these "weapons" you should feel a lot more confident as you enter a new romantic liaison. But, the secret of the longevity of long-term relationships lies in being who you are, in acting transparently, in externalizing your internal dialog and inner voices. In short: if you want your relationships to last, you should express your emotions and concerns on a regular basis. You should knowingly and willingly assume all the risks associated with doing so: of exposing the chinks in your armour; of your vulnerabilities and blind spots being abused, exploited, and leveraged; of being misunderstood, even mocked. But the rewards of being open with your partner (without being naive or gullible) are enormous and multifarious: stronger bonding often results in long-lasting relationships.

Early on you should confer with your intimate partner and inform him of what, to you, constitutes a threat: what types of conduct he should avoid and what modes of communication he should eschew. You should both agree on protocols of communication: fears, needs, triggers, wishes, boundaries, requests, priorities, and preferences should all be shared on a regular basis and in a structured and predictable manner. Remember: structure, predictability, even formality are great antidotes to anxiety.

But there is only that much that your partner can do to ameliorate your mental anguish. You can and should help him in this oft-Herculean task. You can start by using drama to desensitize yourself to your phobia. In your mind imagine and rehearse, in excruciating detail, both the worst-case and best-case scenarios (abandonment in the wake of adultery versus blissful marriage, for instance.)

In these reveries, do not act as an observer: place yourself firmly at the scene of the action and prepare detailed responses within these impromptu plays. At first, this pseudo-theatre may prove agonizing, but the more you exercise your capacity for daydreaming the more you will find yourself immune to abandonment. You may even end up laughing out loud during the more egregious scenes!

Similarly, prepare highly-detailed contingency plans of action for every eventuality, including the various ways in which your relationship can disintegrate. Be prepared for anything and everything, thoroughly and well in advance. Planning equals control and control means lessened dread.

Issues and Goals in the Treatment of Dependent Personality Disorder (Codependence, or Codependency)

ISSUE 1

The patient has alloplastic defenses and an external locus of control. Though she believes that she is in full control of her life, her behavior is mostly reactive and she is buffeted by circumstances and decisions made by other people - hence her tendency to blame the outside world for every misfortune, mishap, and defeat she endures. She rarely takes responsibility for her choices and actions and is frequently surprised and resentful when faced with the consequences of her misconduct.

The patient is convinced that she is worthless and bad, a loser and no-good. She is masochistically self-destructive and self-defeating in her romantic relationships. These propensities are compounded by a predilection to decompensate and act out, sometimes violently, when her defences fail her.

GOAL 1

To develop autoplastic defences and an internal locus of control: to learn to assume responsibility for her actions and refrain from self-destructive and self-defeating behaviors.

ISSUE 2

Having been deprived of it in her childhood, the patient is on a perpetual quest for ideal love: motherly, protective, engulfing, omnipresent, and responsive. Her mate should be handsome, sexy, and should draw attention from and elicit envy. He should be fun to be with and intelligent, although passive, malleable, compliant, and subservient.

Yet, the typical codependent has been exposed only to transactional and conditional love from her parents: love was granted in return for meeting their unrealistic and, therefore, inevitably frustrating expectations.

Such patients resort to fantasy and develop a deficient reality test when it comes to their romantic liaisons. The patient lacks self-awareness and sets conflicting goals for her intimate partners: they are supposed to provide sex, intimacy, companionship and friendship - but also agree to be objectified and to self-deny in order to fulfil their roles in the codependent's "film".

GOAL 2

To develop realistic expectations regarding love, romance, and relationships as well as relationship skills.

ISSUE 3

The narcissistic codependent idealizes her intimate romantic partners and then devalues them. She seeks to "mold" and "sculpt" them to conform to her vision of the relationship. She deprives them of their self-autonomy and makes all decisions for them. In other words: she treats them as objects, she objectifies them. Such a patient is also a verbal and, at times, physical abuser. This impoverishes her relationships and hinders the development of real intimacy and love: there is no real sharing, no discourse, common interests, or joint personal growth.

Owing to the patient's insecure attachment style and abandonment/separation anxiety, she tends to cling to her partner, monopolize his time, smother him, and secure his presence and affection with material gifts (she is a <u>compulsive giver</u>.) As she holds himself worthless and a loser, she finds it hard to believe that any man would attach to her voluntarily, without being bribed or coerced to do so. She tends to suspect her partner's motives and is somewhat paranoid. She is possessive and romantically jealous, though not exceedingly so. This environment tends to foster aversions in her romantic partners.

GOAL 3

To develop a productive and healthy attachment style and learn relationship skills.

ISSUE 4

The codependent's proclaimed desire for stability, safety, predictability, and reliability conflicts with her lifestyle which is itinerant, labile, chaotic, and involves addictive and reckless behaviors. Her need for drama, excitement, and thrill (adrenaline junkie) extends to her romantic relationships. Owing to her low threshold for boredom and multiple depressive, dysphoric, anhedonic, and anergic episodes, she seeks distractions and the partner to provide them. She, therefore, shows a marked preference for men with mental health issues who are likely to lead disorganized lives and to react to her abuse dramatically and theatrically.

GOAL 4

Learn how to choose partners who would bring stability and safety into the relationship and how to interact with them constructively. Learn anger management skills.

ISSUE 5

The narcissistic codependent has strong narcissistic defences, especially when it comes to maintaining her grandiosity with the aid of narcissistic supply. She needs to feel chosen and desired (a flip coin of and antidote to her fear of rejection); be the centre of attention (vicariously, via her intimate partner); and to conform to expectations, values, of judgments or her peer group, relatives, and other role models and reference figures. See: Inverted Narcissist.

GOAL 5

To develop a more realistic assessment of herself and her romantic partners and, thus, reduce her dependence on narcissistic defences and narcissistic supply.

III. The Personal

Narcissists and Personal Attraction: That Thing between a Man and a Woman...

... I lack.

That moist energy, the hungry eyes, the imperceptible tilt of bodies lusting, that magnetism. I do not have it. I do not know the frequency of the silent broadcasts of sexuality. My face is handsome in a man-child way. My features broad but quite agreeable. Sometimes I am rich and powerful, or famous. I can turn on at will a fount of irresistible, immersing, spuriously empathic charm.

Women are curious, even inexorably drawn. But as they inch closer, they sense the void that I am; the howling abyss where a person should have been; the abode of death cloaked in the deceptive hallmarks of an ebullient, exuberant, ostensibly productive life. I am the quintessentially deceptive package, an awry being, a mental alien in an uncanny carnal outfit.

Until a few years back I was able to disguise my illness. I mimicked the behaviours, the intricate messages, the subtle bodily perfumes, the long and longing looks. But now I can't. I am exhausted. These rites of procreation drain me of the energy I need so abundantly in my pursuit of my supply. Freud called it sublimation. I am a prolific author. My seeds are verbal. My passion is abstract. I rarely copulate, once every decade or two, when I am drunk .

In women I induce confusion. They are attracted and then repelled by some essence that they cannot explain, nor name. "He is so unpleasant" - they say, hesitantly - "He is so... violent... and so... disagreeable". My own girlfriends, paramours, and wives struggled with this fetid, repellent emanation. They called me "sick" and "creepy" or "damaged goods." They meant to say that I am not a healthy person altogether, not all there.

The animals we are, women sense my infirmity. I read somewhere that female birds avoid the sickly males in mating season. I am one sickly bird and they skirt me with the hurt perplexity of the frustrated. In this modern world of "what you see is what you get", the narcissist is an exception: false advertising, a diversion, an android of virtual reality with bug-infested programming.

The few women who do possess the audacity and temerity to pursue me with zeal and despite my ominous quiddity thereby unequivocally demonstrate their innate and manifest inferiority and pathology. These odd deviants provoke in me the most aggressive impulses. I am violently repelled by their presbyopic presumptuousness: what makes them think that they have anything that I might need, let alone desire? Whence springs their self-delusion that they automatically hold sway over me by virtue of their genitalia and gender-specific wiles? Can't they tell that I am immune to – nay, revolted by – their ostensible charms and age-old stratagems?

Not long ago, I was still able to control myself, to hide my vile thoughts, to play the social game, to mimetically engage in human intercourse. I can no longer. I am the denuded narcissist - bereft of old defences. This transparency is the ultimate - and psychopathic - act of sheer contempt. People are not even worth maintaining my defences anymore. This frightens women. They sense the danger. Psychic annihilation is often irresistible, the brinkmanship of self-destruction luring. That evil is aesthetic we all know. But it is also so alien, like waking from a nightmare into its continuation in reality.

But I am not an evil man, I am simply indifferent and wish not to be bothered. This schizoid streak conflicts with my narcissism and with my virility. The narcissist devours people, consumes their output, and casts the empty, writhing shells aside. The schizoid avoids them at all costs. As a man, I am very much attracted to the opposite sex. I am imaginative in my fantasies and prone to sexual abandon. But to a schizoid, women are nuisance and annoyance. Obtaining voluntary sex requires too much effort and waste of scarce resources.

Most narcissists go through schizoid phases in their inexorable orbits of gloom and mania. Sometimes the schizoid prevails. A narcissist that is also a schizoid is an unnatural hybrid, a chimera, a shattered personality. The push and pull, the approach and the avoidance, the compulsive search for the drugs that only humans can provide and the no less compulsive urge to avoid them altogether... it is a sorry sight. The narcissist shrivels and withers as the battle is prolonged. He becomes almost psychotic at the tug of war inside him. Alienated even from his False Self by his schizoid disorder, such a narcissist is turned into a gaping black hole, out to suck the vitality of those around him.

So, you see, that thing between a woman and a man - I lack it.

My Woman and I

No woman has ever wanted to have a child with me. It is very telling. Women have children even with incarcerated murderers. I know because I have been to jail with these people. But no woman has ever felt the urge to perpetuate US - the we-ness of she and I.

I was married once and almost married twice but women are very hesitant with me. They definitely do not want anything binding. It is as though they want to maintain all routes of escape clear and available. It is a reversal of the prevailing myth about non-committal males and women huntresses.

But no one wants to hunt a predator.

It is an arduous and eroding task to live with me. I am atrabilious, infinitely pessimistic, bad-tempered, paranoid and sadistic in an absent-minded and indifferent manner. My daily routine is a rigmarole of threats, complaints, hurts, eruptions, moodiness and rage. I rail against slights true and imagined. I alienate people. I humiliate them because this is my only weapon against the humiliation of their indifference to me.

Gradually, wherever I am, my social circle dwindles and then vanishes. Every narcissist is also a schizoid, to some extent. A schizoid is not a misanthrope. He does not necessarily hate people - he simply does not need them. He regards social interactions as a nuisance to be minimized.

I am torn between my need to obtain narcissistic supply (the monopoly on which is held by human beings) - and my fervent wish to be left alone. This wish, in my case, is peppered with contempt and feelings of superiority.

There are fundamental conflicts between dependence and contempt, neediness and devaluation, seeking and avoiding, turning on the charm to attract adulation and being engulfed by wrathful reactions to the most minuscule "provocations". These conflicts lead to rapid cycling between gregariousness and self-imposed ascetic seclusion.

Such an unpredictable but always bilious and festering atmosphere is hardly conducive to love or sex. Gradually, both become extinct. My relationships are hollowed out. Imperceptibly, I switch to a-sexual co-habitation.

But the vitriolic environment that I create is only one hand of the equation. The other hand is the woman herself.

I am heterosexual, so I am attracted to women. But I am simultaneously repelled, horrified, bewitched and provoked by them. I seek to frustrate and humiliate them. Psychodynamically, I am probably visiting upon them my mother's sin - but I think such an instant explanation does the subject great injustice.

Most narcissists I know - myself included - are misogynists. Their sexual and emotional lives are perturbed and chaotic. They are unable to love in any true sense of the word - nor are they capable of developing any measure of intimacy. Lacking empathy, they are incapable of offering to the partner emotional sustenance.

I have been asked many times if I miss loving, whether I would have liked to love and if I am angry with my parents for crippling me so. There is no way I can answer these questions. I never loved. I do not know what is it that I am missing. Observing it from the outside, love seems to me to be a risible pathology. But I am only guessing.

I am not angry for being unable to love. I equate love with weakness. I hate being weak and I hate and despise weak people (and, by implication, the very old and the very young). I do not tolerate stupidity, disease and dependence - and love seems to encompass all three. These are not sour grapes. I really feel this way.

I am an angry man - but not because I never experienced love and probably never will. No, I am angry because I am not as powerful, awe inspiring and successful as I wish to be and as I deserve to be. Because my daydreams refuse so stubbornly to come true. Because I am my worst enemy. And because, in my unmitigated paranoia, I see adversaries plotting everywhere and feel discriminated against and contemptuously ignored. I am angry because I know that I am sick and that my sickness prevents me from realizing even a small fraction of my potential.

My life is a mess as a direct result of my disorder. I am a vagabond, avoiding my creditors, besieged by hostile media in more than one country, hated by one and all. Granted, my disorder also gave me "Malignant Self Love", the rage to write as I do (I am referring to my political essays), a fascinating life and insights a healthy man is unlikely to attain. But I find myself questioning the trade-off ever more often.

But at other times, I imagine myself healthy and I shudder. I cannot conceive of a life in one place with one set of people, doing the same thing, in the same field with one goal within a decades-old game plan. To me, this is death. I am most terrified of boredom and whenever faced with its haunting prospect, I inject drama into my life, or even danger. This is the only way I feel alive.

I guess all the above portrays a lonely wolf. I am a shaky platform, indeed, on which to base a family, or future plans. I know as much. So, I pour wine to both of us, sit back and watch with awe and with amazement the delicate contours of my female partner. I savor every minute. In my experience, it might well be the last.

References and Bibliography

Marriage, Monogamy, and Sexuality

Jackson, Stevi, and Sue Scott. "The personal is still political: Heterosexuality, feminism and monogamy." *Feminism & psychology* 14.1 (2004): 151-157.

Hall, David S. "Sex at dawn: The prehistoric origins of modern sexuality." *Electronic Journal of Human Sexuality* 13 (2010).

Smith, James R., and Lynn G. Smith. "Beyond monogamy: Recent studies of sexual alternatives in marriage." (1974).

Forste, Renata, and Koray Tanfer. "Sexual exclusivity among dating, cohabiting, and married women." *Journal of Marriage and the Family* (1996): 33-47.

Henrich, Joseph, Robert Boyd, and Peter J. Richerson. "The puzzle of monogamous marriage." *Phil. Trans. R. Soc. B* 367.1589 (2012): 657-669.

Bergstrand, Curtis, and Jennifer Blevins Williams. "Today's alternative marriage styles: The case of swingers." *Electronic Journal of Human Sexuality* 3.10 (2000).

Girgis, Sherif, Robert P. George, and Ryan T. Anderson. "What is marriage." *Harv. JL & Pub. Pol'y* 34 (2011): 245.

Calhoun, Cheshire. "Who's Afraid of Polygamous Marriage-Lessons for Same-Sex Marriage Advocacy from the History of Polygamy." *San Diego L. Rev.* 42 (2005): 1023.

Knapp, Jacquelyn J. "Some non-monogamous marriage styles and related attitudes and practices of marriage counselors." *Family Coordinator* (1975): 505-514.

Strassberg, Maura I. "Distinctions of Form or Substance: Monogamy, Polygamy and Same-Sex Marriage." *NCL Rev.* 75 (1996): 1501.

Klesse, Christian. "Polyamory and its 'others': Contesting the terms of non-monogamy." *Sexualities* 9.5 (2006): 565-583.

Courtiol, Alexandre, et al. "Natural and sexual selection in a monogamous historical human population." *Proceedings of the National Academy of Sciences* 109.21 (2012): 8044-8049.

Wellings, Kaye, et al. "Sexual behaviour in context: a global perspective." *The Lancet* 368.9548 (2006): 1706-1728.

Borneman, John. "Caring and being cared for: Displacing marriage, kinship, gender, and sexuality." *The ethics of kinship: Ethnographic inquiries* 1.29 (2001).

Seidman, Steven. *The social construction of sexuality*. New York: Norton, 2003.

Pathological Narcissism and Narcissistic Personality Disorder (NPD)

Alford, C. Fred. Narcissism: Socrates, the Frankfurt School and Psychoanalytic Theory. New Haven and London, Yale University Press, 1988

Devereux, George. Basic Problems of Ethno-Psychiatry. University of Chicago Press, 1980

Fairbairn, W. R. D. An Object Relations Theory of the Personality. New York, Basic Books, 1954

Freud S. Three Essays on the Theory of Sexuality (1905). Standard Edition of the Complete Psychological Works of Sigmund Freud. Vol. 7. London, Hogarth Press, 1964

Freud, S. On Narcissism. Standard Ed. Vol. 14, p. 73-107

Gelder, Michael, Gath, Dennis, Mayou, Richard, Cowen, Philip (Eds.). Oxford Textbook of Psychiatry, third edition, 1996, reprinted 2000. Oxford University Press, Oxford

Goldman, Howard H. (Ed.). Review of General Psychiatry. 4th Ed. London, Prentice Hall International, 1995

Golomb, Elan. Trapped in the Mirror: Adult Children of Narcissists in Their Struggle for Self. Quill, 1995

Greenberg, Jay R. and Mitchell, Stephen A. Object Relations in Psychoanalytic Theory. Cambridge, Mass., Harvard University Press, 1983

Grunberger, Bela. Narcissism: Psychoanalytic Essays. New York, International Universities Press, 1979

Guntrip, Harry. Personality Structure and Human Interaction. New York, International Universities Press, 1961

Horowitz M. J. Sliding Meanings: A Defence against Threat in Narcissistic Personalities. International Journal of Psychoanalytic Psychotherapy, 1975; 4:167

Horovitz M. J. Stress Response Syndromes: PTSD, Grief and Adjustment Disorders. 3rd Ed. New York, NY University Press, 1998

Jacobson, Edith. The Self and the Object World. New York, International Universities Press, 1964

Jung, C.G. Collected Works. G. Adler, M. Fordham and H. Read (Eds.). 21 volumes. Princeton University Press, 1960-1983

Kernberg O. Borderline Conditions and Pathological Narcissism. New York, Jason Aronson, 1975

Klein, Melanie. The Writings of Melanie Klein. Roger Money-Kyrle (Ed.). 4 Vols. New York, Free Press, 1964-75

Kohut H. The Chicago Institute Lectures 1972-1976. Marian and Paul Tolpin (Eds.). Analytic Press, 1998

Kohut M. The Analysis of the Self. New York, International Universities Press, 1971

Lasch, Christopher. The Culture of Narcissism. New York, Warner Books, 1979

Levine, J. D., and Weiss, Rona H. The Dynamics and Treatment of Alcoholism. Jason Aronson, 1994

Lowen, Alexander. Narcissism: Denial of the True Self. Touchstone Books, 1997

Millon, Theodore (and Roger D. Davis, contributor). Disorders of Personality: DSM IV and Beyond. 2nd Ed. New York, John Wiley and Sons, 1995

Millon, Theodore. Personality Disorders in Modern Life. New York, John Wiley and Sons, 2000

Riso, Don Richard. Personality Types: Using the Enneagram for Self-Discovery. Boston: Houghton Mifflin 1987

Roningstam, Elsa F. (Ed.). Disorders of Narcissism: Diagnostic, Clinical, and Empirical Implications. American Psychiatric Press, 1998

Rothstein, Arnold. The Narcissistic Pursuit of Reflection. 2nd revised Ed. New York, International Universities Press, 1984

Schwartz, Lester. Narcissistic Personality Disorders – A Clinical Discussion. Journal of American Psychoanalytic Association – 22 (1974): 292-305

Salant-Schwartz, Nathan. Narcissism and Character Transformation. Inner City Books, 1985 – p. 90-91

Stern, Daniel. The Interpersonal World of the Infant: A View from Psychoanalysis and Developmental Psychology. New York, Basic Books, 1985

Vaknin, Sam. Malignant Self-love: Narcissism Revisited. Prague and Skopje, Narcissus Publications, 1999-2015

Zweig, Paul. The Heresy of Self Love: A Study of Subversive Individualism. New York, Basic Books, 1968

About the Author

Sam Vaknin (http://samvak.tripod.com) is the author of Malignant Self-Love: Narcissism Revisited and After the Rain - How the West Lost the East, as well as many other books and ebooks about topics in psychology, relationships, philosophy, economics, and international affairs.

He is the Editor-in-Chief of Global Politician and served as a columnist for Central Europe Review, PopMatters, eBookWeb , and Bellaonline, and as a United Press International (UPI) Senior Business Correspondent. He was the editor of mental health and Central East Europe categories in The Open Directory and Suite101.

Visit Sam's Web site at http://www.narcissistic-abuse.com

Work on Narcissism

I am the author of Malignant Self-love: Narcissism Revisited, the pioneering work about narcissistic abuse, now in its 10th, DSM-V compatible revision. My work is quoted in well over 1000 scholarly publications and in over 5000 books (partial list here). **My Narcissists, Psychopaths, and Abuse YouTube channel and my other channels have more than 14.1 million views and 50,000 subscribers.**

The Web site "Malignant Self-love: Narcissism Revisited" had been, for many years, an Open Directory Cool Site and is a Psych-UK recommended Site.

I am *not a mental health professional* though I am certified in psychological counseling techniques by Brainbench.

I served as the editor of Mental Health Disorders categories in the Open Directory Project and on Mentalhelp.net. I maintain my own Websites about the Narcissistic Personality Disorder (NPD) and about relationships with abusive narcissists and psychopaths here and in HealthyPlace.

You can read my work on many other Web sites: Mental Health Matters, Mental Health Sanctuary, Mental Health Today, Kathi's Mental Health Review and others. I write a column for Bellaonline on Narcissism and Abusive Relationships and am a frequent contributor to Websites such as Self-growth.com and Bizymoms (where I am an expert on personality disorders).

I served as the author of the Personality Disorders topic, Narcissistic Personality Disorder topic, the Verbal and Emotional Abuse topic, and the Spousal Abuse and Domestic Violence topic, all four on Suite101. I am the moderator of the Narcissistic Abuse Study List , the Toxic Relationships Study List, and other mailing lists with a total of c. 20,000 members. I also publish a bi-weekly Abusive Relationships Newsletter.

You can view my biography here.

Printed in Germany
by Amazon Distribution
GmbH, Leipzig